GOOGLE CLASSROOM

THE DEFINITIVE GUIDE FOR
TEACHERS ABOUT HOW TO USE
DIGITAL CLASSROOM AND
IMPROVE THE QUALITY OF YOUR
LESSONS. 2020 EDITION

ANDREW SUTHERLAND

Table Of Contents

INTRODUCTION 6

CHAPTER 1 INTRODUCTION TO GOOGLE CLASSROOM 10

WHAT IS IT? 10
WHAT ARE THE NEW UPDATES? 13
BENEFITS OF GOOGLE CLASSROOM FOR EVERYONE!................... 16

CHAPTER 2 INTRODUCTION TO GOOGLE DRIVE AND DOCS 23

THE BASICS OF GOOGLE DRIVE: 25
THE ADVANCED FEATURES OF GOOGLE DRIVE:...................... 26
GETTING STARTED.. 28
GOOGLE DOCS... 34
ADDING FILES IN YOUR GOOGLE DRIVE:............................ 36
CONVERTING THE NON-NATIVE (UPLOADED) DOCUMENTS TO GOOGLE DOCS:
.... 38

CHAPTER 3 INTRODUCTION TO GOOGLE FORMS 41

WHERE ARE THEY STORED? 41
CREATING A GOOGLE FORM.. 42
STYLING YOUR GOOGLE FORM 44
QUESTION SETTINGS/OPTIONS 54

CHAPTER 4 GETTING STARTED FOR TEACHER..............................58

SETTING UP THE CLASSROOM...................................... 58
DAILY USE OF CLASSROOM 60
THINGS CLASSROOM DOESN'T DO.................................. 61
WHAT ELSE CAN I DO WITH GOOGLE CLASSROOM? 62

CHAPTER 5 GETTING STARTED FOR STUDENT 70

SIGNING IN.. 71
VIEWING THE CLASS RESOURCE PAGE.............................. 72
VIEWING AN ARCHIVED CLASS..................................... 73
VIEWING THE CLASS CALENDAR.................................... 74
SETTING UP YOUR MOBILE NOTIFICATIONS 76
HOW TO CHANGE YOUR ACCOUNT SETTINGS 79

CHAPTER 6 TIPS FOR DIFFERENTIATION AND TOOLS TO USE.......81

TIPS FOR TEACHERS 81
TIPS FOR STUDENTS 85

CHAPTER 7 DEMONSTRATIONS OF LEARNING 91

TEACHING MATH..91
TEACH PROGRAMMING 94
TEACHING SCIENCE...94
TEACHING WRITING & READING...96
TEACHING PHYSICAL EDUCATION 98
OTHER TEACHING METHODS TO USE 100

CHAPTER 8 THINGS YOU CAN DO WITH GOOGLE CLASSROOM .. 103

SHARING CONTENT WITH THE CLASS...103
ASSIGNMENT FUN..105
CREATING QUIZZES AND ASSIGNMENTS 106
MANAGE DIFFERENT CLASSES..107
CREATING RESOURCES PAGE..108

CHAPTER 9 GUIDELINES & SUGGESTIONS FOR CLASSROOM MANAGEMENT AND INSTRUCTIONAL FORMS................................. 109

CHAPTER 10 EXAMPLE OF GOOGLE FORM USES............................ 117

USES FOR GOOGLE FORMS IN THE CLASSROOM 117
EXAMPLE OF GOOGLE FORM USES 120

CHAPTER 11 FAQS ABOUT GOOGLE CLASSROOM 129

IS IT EASY TO GET STARTED WITH GOOGLE CLASSROOM? 129
HOW ARE APPS FOR EDUCATION AND CLASSROOM CONNECTED? 130
DOES IT COST TO USE GOOGLE CLASSROOM? 131
CAN I STILL USE CLASSROOM IF IT IS DISABLED ON MY DOMAIN?.............131
DO I NEED TO HAVE GMAIL ENABLED TO USE CLASSROOM? 132
WILL I HAVE TO WORK WITH ADS ON GOOGLE CLASSROOM? 132
IF I HAVE A DISABILITY, AM I ABLE TO USE GOOGLE CLASSROOM? 133

CHAPTER 12 ORGANIZING STUDENTS PROJECTS 135

ORGANIZING ASSIGNMENTS 141
HOW STUDENTS ACCESS ASSIGNMENTS 144
GRADING ASSIGNMENTS 146
GRADING TIPS 150

CONCLUSION... 152

Introduction

G oogle Classroom is a new tool that teachers and students can use in an educational setting. It blends the different apps from Google to help schools in their goal of education. Teachers can create a classroom and invite all their students to join. During the year, homework assignments, discussion questions, and even testing can be completed on the Google Classroom platform, making it easier for students to complete their work even outside the classroom.

This platform has several different uses. Many teachers who conduct online classes have turned to using Google Classroom because it allows them to easily post up reading material and assignments as well as the required class participation (discussions) and other information that the students need. Since most students can use Google and the platform is free, this is a great way to get online courses started.

Regular classrooms that meet each day can use this information as well. Students inside the classroom can take tests through the platform, get together in groups and answer questions for discussion, and even submit answers all in one place. When the teacher assigns homework, it will be waiting on the platform for the students once they get home.

Google Classroom is a great way to make education more fun and to take out some of the hassles that slow down learning in the classroom. Students can easily use this platform to ask their questions or to complete assignments, and there is no need to waste time printing out packets for each student or handing out assignments in the classroom. Everything is in one place so the students can spend more time learning!

The great thing about Google Classroom is that it ties together many of the other products from Google to provide a paperless system for educational institutions to use. You will be able to use Google Drive to create and distribute assignments, and Gmail is good for sending information to the students. Google Calendar helps the students know when different assignments are due and even when other important events, such as tests, will occur. Get class can also use Google Docs to submit assignments and the teacher can then view and grade the homework.

All of these work together to make things easier for students and teachers. Communication is done just through regular emails and it takes just a few seconds for the teacher to create assignments and for students to submit their work. Also, Google Classroom does not use ads in the program so no one has to worry about this interfering with the work or about Google collecting private information.

Google Drive is going to be the main point of contact for assignments with Google Classroom. Teachers can either look at documents the students have uploaded, and grade from

there, or they can upload a template that each student can change and resubmit as their own. This can be helpful if the teacher needs a worksheet or discussion questions answered for homework. Also, if the student needs to attach supporting documents, this can easily be done in Google Drive as well.

Teachers can choose the way that they would like to grade in this platform. One option is just to have the students submit the work and teachers can choose to grade by marking answers correct or not before sending the information back. On other assignments, such as projects that will take some time or for essays, the teacher can track progress, make edits, and even grade with notes and send it back for revisions.

As a teacher, you may be curious as to why you would want to go with Google Classroom rather than working with your personal account. It is possible to work with your personal account in the classroom, but you do not get the results that you are looking for. For example, with a personal account, you will have to worry about sending through bulky emails if you are sending out attachments. The due dates that you pick are not going to upload to Google Calendars, and information can easily get lost for students if it isn't all put in the same place.

It is possible to work with your own personal account, but in reality, Google Classroom is one of the best options to help you to manage your classroom. This platform is all about being used for educational purposes. It doesn't cost anything to get started and it can save most teachers around 52 hours of work time each year, which is nothing to sneeze at. Add in that Google Classroom rarely experiences any downtime and they have a great customer support system, and this is one of the best options for you to go with.

If you just want to send a few emails back and forth between your students and you aren't interested in moving any of your classrooms online, your personal account with Gmail is probably going to be just fine. On the other hand, if you are interested in moving some or a lot of your classroom online and you want to make sure that it is a platform that is really easy for your students to get on and use, then Google Classroom is the right option for you.

Introduction to Google Classroom

The first thing you might ask is well, what is Google Classroom. We will discuss here in this chapter what Google Classroom is, and some of the new upgrades that were recently done to Google Classroom so that you can better understand the different aspects of Google Classroom.

What Is It?

Google Classroom is a web service that was developed by Google for educators and schools with the purpose of making assignments paperless and to streamline the file sharing system between students and teachers. Essentially, this uses the entire Google ecosystem, such as Google docs, slides and sheets for writing and presentation, the Gmail communication system, and for scheduling, you use Google calendar. Students can join the classes their teachers have made with the use of a private code, or are automatically imported from the domain. Every single class is separated based on folders within the drive, students can put work in there, and teachers can grade it. It essentially is like putting your entire classroom on a computer, and it does help streamline both the education, and the communication between the teachers, and the students alike.

The coolest part about this, is that if you don't want to talk on a computer or use a computer, there are mobile apps for both Android and Apple devices that lets students do assignments on their device, even put photos on there, share different apps and files, and also access information on their devices both online and offline. Even with this, teachers can contact and speak to students, they can monitor how a student is doing, and once they are graded, teachers can go back and add comments to their work on order to ensure that students have the best education possible.

The system actually allows more administrative tasks to be done in an effective manner. Because of the G suite for education, it makes tasks that are otherwise boring much faster. It works wherever you are, teacher or student, whether it be from any computer, any mobile device, or whatever, and it allows teachers to have access to the assignments that are there, the course materials they need, and all of the feedback in one awesome place.

The coolest part about this is that it is free. It's free for schools that have signed up for G suite for education, and like with any of the tools the classroom meets one of the highest standards that's out there, and it's a super fun system, and it is free, and works better than most free software that's out there.

Another great thing about this, is that I t allows feedback to come back to the student right away. Educators are able to track the progress of a student, and let them know how they are doing. More focus can be put on making sure that the student gets it, which is something that many students want to have. The cool thing about this is how integrative this is to the workplace for students, and teachers will be able to help in a much timelier manner. Plus, it allows for a more personalized construction, and it will allow students to have a better time learning subjects as well.

For teachers and students, it will save them time, effort, paper, and it will allow teachers to create a better environment for assignments and quizzes, and you can always talk to parent s and guardians with this. You can copy and tweak assignments as well one to another, and control multiple classes as well, which is great if you are looking to truly master this type of system. It is great for students and teachers alike, and allows for a collaborative system that will in turn create a better and more immersive system than you have thought possible.

Many praise Google drive because of the accessibility of the devices, the utilization of Google drive, and the ability to go paperless. But, it does have the disadvantage of little support for external services, although that's changing, the lack of auto quizzes, and also the lack of any live chatting that teachers can use for feedback, but it's obvious that Google is looking to update, so we may get to see these changes sooner than ever.

What are the New Updates?

There are always new updates happening, and as a teacher or student, it is important to consider these updates. You actually are going to get some new and immersive updates to classroom that can ultimately help you.

One of the newest updates actually just came out in December of 2018 and that is the Classroom Gradebook. Which is a beta, but if you as a teacher want to edit and look at grades, share them with the students, or even create weighted grades and calculations on either a mobile or desktop version, you'll be able to fix the grades on the fly. You'll need to utilize the beta and sign up for this, but there is a lot of support that's available for this.

With this, you can use the tool that helps with trading, and this can be used with videos, various PDFs, and also the documents that you need. You can also put the assignments together by modules and units. You can use this to engage with students so you can give the students feedback on their items, and what can be improved upon, allowing for more engagement.

You can also determine where the documents come from. For example, it can be used with google docs, but you can also use it for other documents as well in order to help improve feedback to students.

Then there is the people page. In the past, you'd go to the students page to message students and guardians, and the teaches would be in the about page, but now, if you want to see everyone, whether they be teachers, co-teachers, guardians, or students, you can now do it all under the people tab, which is right next to the classwork page. You can email, remove, and for students mute or for teachers make them a class owner, which affects what they can do for the class.

There is also the student selector, which is great if you want to call on students that you want to have discuss something. This is a feature on android, and from this, teachers can choose a random student, especially in the case of answering. While students may not enjoy this, this new feature allows for more participation, and if you do not want to think too much on who to choose for what, this is a way to facilitate that. Finally, let's discuss the new settings page. In the past, all of the functions were in different locations, but, the new settings page all puts it in a gear that is located near the top right location whenever you go to the class. Essentially, when you go to the menu, you choose that, and you are given many different options. In this, you can choose the class details, which you can use a pencil in order to edit and change, and you can even change the location, the description, or even where classes meet. You also can get the class code here, which allows you to give this to the students if they have to self-enroll within the class. You also can control what students do on the stream page here, whether they are allowed to post, place comments only, or it is just a place for teachers to do announcements. You can also control whatever gets deleted here, which is good if you notice when someone posts comments or posts that aren't appropriate for the class or even for school. Finally, you can find out the information from the parents here, and the guardian summaries that can ultimately be changed if you feel like you need to add more information. It has a separate settings area that teachers can look at and consult, in order to help facilitate the use. It also allows you to have a less cluttered about page and in turn will allow for more resources to be used in the future. It does create a great difference, and ultimately, is something that allows for some great changes to Google Classroom.

The Google Classroom is a great addition to any school, and if you have been confused as to what it can totally do, you can read all about it in the ensuing chapters. Nevertheless, the purpose of this chapter is to give you an idea of what Google Classroom is, so that you are not confused anymore, and in turn, can understand it even better than before.

Benefits of Google Classroom for Everyone!

For many educators, they may see that it's a great system, but who else can benefit from this? Well, let's talk about how it benefits everyone, including teachers, students, and parents. This chapter will tell you all about the benefits of Google Classroom for everyone, and why it matters.

Less Paperwork!

This is a benefit for everyone. Do you as a teacher tend to have worksheets that students may come to you days later to tell you that they lost it? Or maybe you need a new roll book for attendance? Or maybe you have this worksheet that you've found, but don't want to waste valuable class time trying to copy it? Or maybe you just don't want to deal with papers upon papers? If you're sick of it, then Google Classroom is for you. With this system, you can create worksheets in the Google drive, share it to the class, or even make a form for students to fill out. You can use the "share to classroom" feature in order to share new and valuable items to the classroom. Not only that, you can create a digital logbook which in turn will save you lots of paper. If you want to save yourself stress, and save the environment as well, then Google Classroom is the way to go, because it uses so much less energy. Everyone can be on the same page, and creates a collaboration not seen before.

Managing Workflow

If you have assignments that involve having them all collected at once, then you should start using Google Classroom. This actually can tell you in real-time the progress of a student to see who's done and not done, allowing you to see the status of students who are missing items, and you can timestamp everything, so you won't allow late work to slide. For teachers as well, you can actually go to the screen that says student work, and see the progress on there, since it's actually all tied into Google docs or slides. It allows you to see any revisions that you see as well, and you can see the student production too. That way, everyone is watched, and you can help with the student's progress as needed.

Allows the use of Online Learning Platforms

One nice thing about Google Classroom is that it's so easy. For many students, when they get to college, they may be confused by the idea of degree work online. However, online classes are super popular, so if you want to get them ahead of the game, you should expose them to what it's like to have an online-only education. Google classroom is a great way to do this, because it's super easy for everyone, and most students love it, since everything is there.

Gets better Conversations going

Sometimes, it's very awkward trying to ask questions, and students are either too nervous to speak, or maybe they don't want to, or they often are stunted on deepening though. But, did you know that you could get more engagement from students in a better way through the use of Google Classroom. Just posting a question in the questions area will get students to comment. The best part, is other students can comment there, and it can deepen the way students do learn the coursework, and it can make your life easier. Even the most socially awkward of students will benefit from this, because it's easier to say things online than in person, and it can make a world of a difference in the long run.

Easy Support

One thing that's great about this, is that if you're a teacher or an administrator, and don't know how to use this, you can get the help that you need. With G suite, you'll be able to use Google Classroom easily with their helpful how-to software, set permissions, have some support at all times of the day, and you actually can use this software and protect the data and classes. It's a secure software that really will help you, and ultimately will really make your classroom easier to manage. The support can be directly with another person, or you can view some of the tutorials that you may be interested in if you're looking to get better with this site and interface, this is ultimately the way to go. You can use a lot of different help tools in order to really benefit from this.

Can't Lose Work Anymore

If you're a teacher, chances are you've had to deal with the lost work excuses. Students lose work when it's on paper, or it involves a physical object. But, did you know that with this system, it actually eliminates the chances of you losing it. Since Google classroom eliminates the consumption of paper, so long as you've got access to the internet, you'll be okay, and ultimately, it actually will save your district a ton of money on paper. It's quite nice, and it does the job.

Along with that, since it is cloud-based, no matter what computer you're on, you'll be able to access your work. If you have everything on a cloud, it's based off an internet connection rather than a hard drive. You may have heard the excuse from a student that they had a hard drive failure, which is why they couldn't save it or turn it in. but with Google Classroom, it actually can be accessed through all devices, and students can work wherever they are, not have to worry about a flash drive not reading or losing your work, and it eliminates the uses of emails constantly. Plus, all of this saves to the drive immediately, so if there is a computer hiccup, you don't have to worry about losing progress or anything. You don't have to hear the excuse that the computer crashed, or you left the flash drive at home, since you're essentially going to be able to access everything through the internet.

Apps Galore

Google Classroom functions well on a mobile device, which means that you can take this on the go as well. Lots of times, students will make the excuse of they weren't on the computer or saw the assignment, but if they have a phone, you download the app, and you get announcements and various assignments that are posted, so you can stay on top of these. Teachers as well can post in real time any of the assignments that they need, through the app or the sharing support with this, and it's super convenient, and makes your life as a teacher that much easier.

Ease of Workflow

The nice thing about this, is that with the interface, you can add on some products that sync over with Google Classroom, and you can put extra add-ons and apps within this so that you've got a full-on classroom environment. You can track the trends, users, and even students, and administrators of the Google Classroom platform will give students and teachers a better platform over time. Plus, this is always updating, so you'll have the support that you want to.

Real time feedback

One thing that's super nice about this platform, is the fact that teachers can give feedback right away. With each assignment uploaded, the teacher can go through, make some notes, and then give the students feedback that they want. They can reach out immediately if the student is struggling and work with them as needed.

Can Upload Resources

If you have students that need extra copies, you as a teacher don't need to worry about that. What you do, is upload the forms for assignments straight into Google Classroom, and from there, the students can take control over this. If a student misses an assignment, tell them it's in Google Classroom, and from there, you can have students check that whenever possible. It's quite simple.

Saves you SO Much money

One thing that is really nice about this, is the price of Google Classroom. It's free. It saves you a ton of money since everything is paperless and on a drive. You can install free apps on this to really help you get the most out of this, and you'll be able to easily, and without fail, create the lesson plans that you want, and the classroom you desire. It's quite nice, and you can differentiate all of these between classes too. Plus, with constant improvements, it's always growing.

Google Classroom is the future, and you'll be able to easily and without fail really make it better for every student. You don't have to worry about students falling behind, but instead, you'll be able to create a better learning environment that will make everything better.

Introduction to Google Drive and Docs

I n today's world of online working and storage, manual paper storage and file keeping are no more in the business. Almost all of the work being done by people around is now being stored on various online mediums like a cloud.

But when we talk about the most authentic, reliable and efficient storage domain, then Google Drive is surely the king. Although you hear the name Google Drive whenever the storage purpose is in question but Google Drive is much more than mere storage.

By incorporating the enhanced ability, it enables the creation and editing of various categories of file types including files, photos, videos and PDF documents. If you think about its enhanced capability then it is the Drop Box and the Microsoft Office, combined at one place.

And side by side the enhanced features of collaboration and sharing documents, presentations and spreadsheets among all the users of Google drive is surely a plus point.

One of the major reasons for such a heightened fame enjoyed by Google Drive is its extensive storage space. The users for the Google Apps receive at a minimum of 30 GBs for unified storage in order to be used for Drive, Gmail, and Google+ photos.

This so for the regular users but in case you are availing the access over Google Apps then you can get the boundless capacity which equals around 1TB storage capacity. The particular storage entails only files which have not been converted to Spreadsheets, Google Docs, or Presentations.

If you are working on some non-native types of files including the PowerPoint or Microsoft Word then you can convert them to Google document by just a dragging function available over the drive. Here are some of the most basic introductory remarks and information which you must know before using Google drive.

Although the endless limits of Google Drive will take some time to get familiar with entire features yet you need to know as much as possible so that the real benefit can be achieved from this well-crafted Drive. Start with the basic features and you can easily master the higher ones.

The Basics of Google Drive:

The Basic features of Google Drive are the ones which almost every user will need at some point in time. So, knowing them is like a license to start up your use of Google Drive.

- **Set Up**

It is related to getting the introduction for setting up and efficient use of Google Drive.

- **Organize**

These organizing tips will help the user to consolidate the Google Drive in such a way that all the documents are easy to reach and navigate. For example, you can learn the way of adding a single file to different folders.

- **Share**

This will entail the basic working for sharing of some item on the Google Drive of one user over the Google drive of other users. You can also learn to restrict the downloading features of the shared files.

- **Delete**

This will entail the process applied for deleting a file placed on the Google Drive. You can also learn to restore the deleted file.

The Advanced Features of Google Drive:

Some of the sophisticated and advanced actions include:

- **Advanced Search**

The advanced search operators of Google Drive are highly useful when the user is navigating some broader and populated Drive library.

- **View Revision History**

This feature enables the user view and effectively manages the changes which have been made to the files located on Google Drive.

- **Edit Files in Google Drive (Microsoft Files)**

The user can easily edit Microsoft files in such a way that they are eventually converted into the native Google Drive files

- **Attaching Files to an Email**

There is also an option of quickly adding the files stored in Google Drive in the email.

- **Adding a Drive Image as the Email Signature:**

Google Drive's additional capability allows you to add an image in the email signature. You can use any of the images which have been stored in the Drive. You can also learn to create the enhanced features like the signatures for company email.

- **Using Drive for Image Host**

Google Drive also entails the additional feature of hosting some image kept on Google Drive. Eventually, the image can be either be linked or directly used on the website.

- **Adding Subtitles for Videos in Google Drive**

If you have stored some videos in the Google Drive, you can also use the enhanced features of Google drive to place Subtitles on the video.

- **Managing Changes to Non-Native Files**

This enhanced feature allows the user to keep a track of all those amendments and changes which have been made to the non-native files. This also ensures that the users with whom the file is shared can only see the changed or updated file.

- **Allowing Backup for Google+ Photos**

Google Drive also keeps a backup for all the photos which the user posts on Google+.

- **Some special features for Admins:**

As Google Drive enables plenty of domain data to get stored by all the users so it also enables the Google Apps Admins to keep a check on the security of the domain Drive.

- **Drive Security for Apps Admins**

Google Drive provides all the essential processes and related tools for Admins so that they can eventually make up a secured domain.

- **Confirmation of Drive Compliance**

The feature named Better Cloud enables the Admins to scan the domain's Drive to explore the SSNs, credit card numbers and some other form of secured information and modify and monitor the settings related to the sharing of the documents.

Getting Started

In this step, you will get the most basic information for starting on with Google Drive so that the endless possibilities of this Drive can be explored in the best possible way.

Getting Access to Google Drive:

1. There can be many different methods to access the Google Drive, out of which the easiest is to use a Chrome browser. After clicking Chrome, click on a browser or on the new tab. Here you will find the page shown below. Just select the logo for Google Drive which will direct you to the website for Google Drive.

2. In case one does not have the Chrome browser then adding the appropriate URL in the search bar will also direct the user to get access to the Google Drive, as shown below:

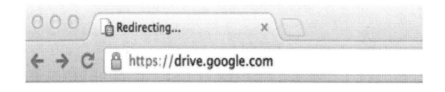

3. There can be another method for accessing Google Drive which is by searching over the Google for Google Drive.

Interface of Google Drive:

The Google Drive entails the following interface: The "My Drive" is actually in synchronization with the desktop of the user.

All of the folders appearing under My Drive will be similar to the ones which are residing within the desktop. You can use the Drag Drop function to put any of the files from the internet to "My Drive".

Desktop Application for Google Drive

When the initial login for the Google Drive will be made, it will prompt the user to download the application for the desktop. You will need to click on the Download option.

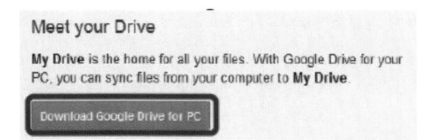

Next, click "Accept and Install"

Next, click on the "Save File" icon for opening the download and proceed to "Run". It will automatically administer you to the necessary steps for downloading.

After downloading the Drive, the next step is to get signed in with a Google account. In order to start the synchronization of Google Documents with Google drive click to "Start Sync".

After this step, the Google Drive will be one of the options for saving the files. You will get a shortcut for Drive over the desktop. You can also apply a Drag- Drop function to directly add files to the drive for internet or some other source.

Google Drive over the Web

- There is an arrow on the left side of "My Drive", which is used to expand the Drive and show all the folders which have been synchronized with the Google Drive. Select any of the folders and its content will be displayed at the right of the screen.

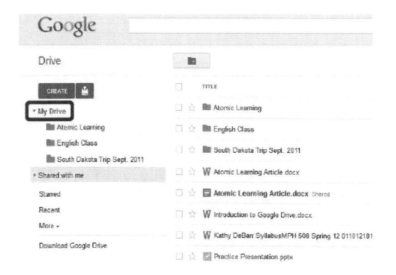

- In case you add some folder or file over the desktop, it will automatically become part of the Drive.

- Adding to folders in the "My drive" is also possible. First of all, click "Create "and from the drop down options and select the "Folders" options.

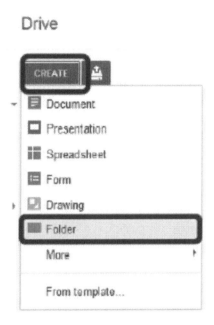

- Add some name to the new folder and it will become part of my drive folders just like the previous ones.

Google Docs

Google Docs can be thought of as the online version of PowerPoint, Microsoft Word, and Excel. In the language of Google Docs, you will call them Presentation, Google Document, and Spreadsheet respectively.

Once the registration process is completed the user is then directed to the following page of Google Drive.

As indicated in the picture, the Google Drive panel is further divided into three major parts.

- Towards the left, you can see the folder view which contains all those files which are present as shared files, modified files as well as the files starred by the user

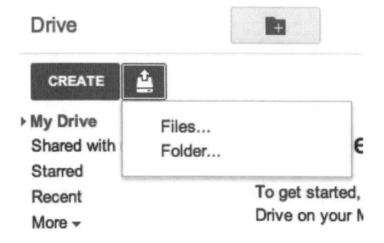

- Over the top lies the menu bar which carries all the options including the creation of new folders, sorting of files, various viewing and setting option.

- The center area of the drive is the one which carries all files available in the Drive. These files will all be displayed in this center portion. Initially, when the user will just start with the drive and there will be no files in his or her drive then this central part will be occupied with the information regarding Google Drive.

Adding files in your Google Drive:

Two different methods can be applied in order to create files for your Google drive.

- The first method relates to the creation of an empty file from the very beginning. It is accomplished by clicking on the button named "Create".

- The second method entails an uploading of the existing file over the Drive and working with it afterward. For this method, you will click the Hard disk icon having arrow button as well as the choose file icon and create button

You will come across an upload file panel. Now browse for the specific file which you intend to upload to the Google Drive. Click on the specific file and select upload. When this process will be completed, you will get the specific panel which is shown below:

Now when you will close the panel for the file upload, the Google drive will show that particular file in the drive.

The picture below depicts the same procedure in which the file which we uploaded in previous steps can be seen in the central part of the drive, which is fixed for the files available in the Drive.

Converting the non-native (uploaded) documents to Google Docs:

You can see in the previous steps that the file which was uploaded to the Google Drive was having the icon "W" with it.

It indicates that although it is residing in your Google Drive, yet it is still in the Microsoft Document form and is not in the Google Doc form.

In this part of the book, we will deal with conversion of a document to Google Doc form, which is necessary in order to make modifications and editing in the document.

You can see it if you click on the file which you have uploaded to the drive. Opening a document in the original form will not let you make any changes in the document. For making it editable and compatible with the Google Drive you need to make a Google Doc version of it.

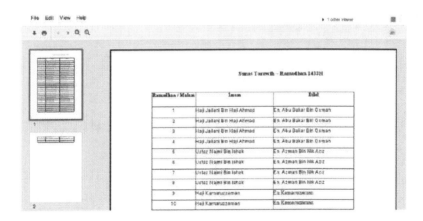

Click on "File" then "Open With" and then select "Google Docs".

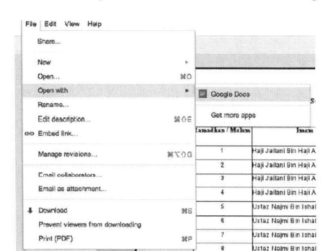

After this step, the original file uploaded in the Word format will appear as Google Docs. You can then open this file in a separate editor.

Any kind of modifications and editing can easily be done now on this Google Doc file. Now if you just close the editor tab and go to the home page of Google Drive you can easily see that there will be two separate files in the field area.

One will be the original version of the file which was uploaded in the first step. The second will be the one which you just converted into the Google Doc format.

In this case, one thing which is important to remember is that the modifications will be stored in the Google Doc file so if you want to use the changed and modified file you will need to click the Google Doc version.

The word format file will reside as it was in the original format at the time of uploading. This should be dealt with care while considering official and corporate matters.

Introduction to Google Forms

G oogle forms is one of the features of Google drive, alongside, Google Docs, Google Sheet, etc. Google drive is a product of Google.

Where are They Stored?

The first thing you'll need to create a google form is a Gmail account. You must be signed in to your Gmail account before you can create a google form. Also note that any google form you create is linked to the Gmail account that is signed in as at the time you created the google form.

All your google forms are saved on your Google drive. There is a Google drive for every Gmail account created, with 15Gb of free storage space which can be expanded upon request. That's why you need to know the Gmail address you are signed in to before creating your Google forms.

Creating a Google Form

To create a new Google form, you'll need;

1. A Gmail address

2. A browser

3. An internet connection

Note: Most of the explanations here are accompanied with laptop/desktop images, and may differ when creating google forms with mobile phones.

Step 1

Open your browser, and type the URL (https://google.com/forms)

Step 2

Click on "Blank quiz". But If you aren't creating a quiz, just a normal form that won't require grading, you should click on just "Blank".

Step 3

If you clicked on "Blank", you should see an empty form like the one below. Click on the "untitled form" at the top left corner of the form, and change to a more suitable title. However, this title is only the name given to the form for storage purpose.

The "untitled form" (above form description) on the white field will automatically change to the title you gave above. You may however still change this title, as it is the name your students will see when filling your form.

Step 4

Form description: You can use this field to give instructions to your students such as "Answer all questions in this quiz" or "Ensure you complete this test alone and submit before Monday".

Styling Your Google Form

Styling your Google form is probably one of the most neglected part of creating a google form, but for teachers, this is a point of attraction. Follow the steps below to style your google form.

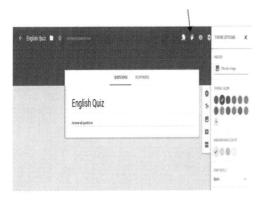

Step 1
Click on the theme/palette symbol at the top right corner of the form to change the theme of the form. With this palette, you can also change the background color and font style of your form.

Step 2

Click on "choose image to change the header of your form. A box will open with preinstalled images to choose from for your header (see image below). Or you can click on "upload photos" to select a picture from your computer.

Click here to change theme color if you are not using an image for the header

Click here to change the font style of your form.

Getting Started With Asking Questions

The Form template has one question field already on it when it opens. To add more questions, click on the + sign in the right tool box.

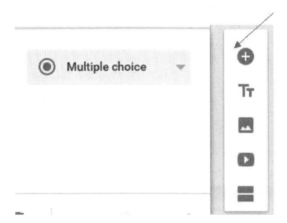

The default field is set up for a Multiple-Choice question. To change the question type, click on the down-arrow (beside multiple choice) to reveal the drop-down menu. YOU SHOULD ALWAYS CREATE A SHORT ANSWER FIELD FIRST FOR THE STUDENT'S NAME. Adding the NAME field first BEFORE your questions are added will place the student's name in the FIRST column of the spreadsheet that shows student's answers/responses (spreadsheet will be explained later).

These are the different question types available.

The question type selections are –

Short Answer - Works well for short, written text responses. Best for responses that won't require long text. Ex. – First Name; last name; School; Class; Age; Short sentences; short phrases; spelling tests.

Paragraph - This question type works well for longer, written text responses/answers. Ex. – Essay responses; responses to writing prompts; summaries.

Multiple Choice - Respondents pick one option from choices. Multiple choice question type can also be used to create true/false responses by labeling one choice true and one choice false. Google form automatically creates options for you in multiple choice based on its understanding of your question. You may choose to use it or create yours. You create more options by clicking the "Add option" NOT "Add other".

Checkboxes - - This question type lets respondents pick as many options as they'd like. In other words, when there may be more than one answer. An example of the use of this question type could be "choose all that apply".

Dropdown - This question type works well when there is a long list of choice options, e.g. State of Origin, Nationality, etc. This question type also works well for sequencing.

File Upload: This type allows the student upload certain documents such as pictures or videos. You can select the different document formats that the student can upload and the maximum file size. This feature is valuable when you want your students to submit their workings or when requesting for CVs.

Linear Scale - This question type lets the respondent rank something along a designated scale of numbers. Scales are good to use for rubrics, peer and general evaluations. The highest number on the scale rating question type is 10, while the least is 0. Most people use 1-5 as their range. 1 can represent Poor while 5 can represent Excellent.

Multiple-Choice Grid - a grid can work as a scale for more than one question and response. If used as a scale, it takes up less space on a form than placing a scale for each question. You can also create a grid for multiple choice responses.

Checkbox Choice Grid: This works the same as multiple choice grid, except that more than one option can be chosen. You can however limit the response to "one choice per column".

Date – This field is to insert a date into your Form. By default, a calendar pops up when this field is to be filled. This option is suitable for questions like Date of Birth.

Time – This field enables the respondent to insert the time into your Form.

QUESTION TOOLBOX

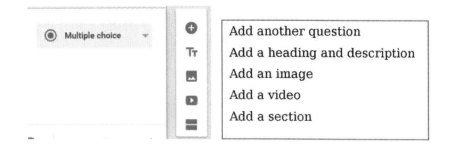

You're probably already familiar with what the + sign does. You use it to add new questions to your forms. The others are explained briefly below.

Heading & Description (TT)

This feature is used to break your quiz into thematic chunks. Each "chunk" can then be labeled with a heading, and a description can be added for instructions. For example, if I were giving a Form quiz on English Language, I may label one part of the quiz with the heading, Grammar, and another part with

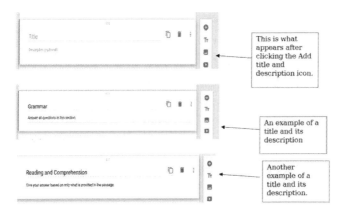

Reading and Comprehension.

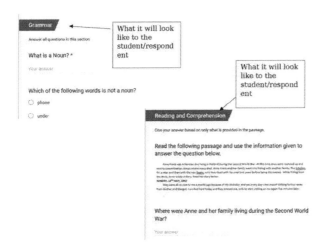

Adding an Image

You can insert images into your Form to use as writing prompts. For example, if I were a Biology teacher (which I certainly am not), and I wanted to give a quiz based on a topic I recently taught such as Flowering plant. I could get a picture of the plant, with certain parts already labelled.

Steps: Click on add image; a dialogue box opens; select "chose an image to upload"; After selecting the image, add title to the image such as Parts of a Flowering Plant (this title is different from the "title and description learnt" above). The image can be resized (smaller or bigger). It can also be aligned to the left, right, or center, by clicking on the 3 dots at the top-left side of the image.

You could then "add a question" accompanying the image such as "which of the following is the part labelled B? (of cos, you already know this should be a multiple-choice question).

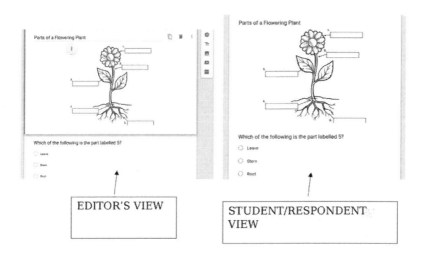

If you have the direct website link to the image, you can also paste it in the URL field, and it will be automatically uploaded.

Adding a Video

You can add a YouTube video for instructional purposes. Once you've selected the add video option, you can select a video from your computer just like it was explained for adding pictures. Alternatively, you can search YouTube for the particular video you want within the dialog box, or paste in a direct URL to the YouTube video. A question can then follow, as we learnt in "adding image".

Adding a Section

Adding sections lets you break down your quiz into separate pages, with a NEXT button to move to the next Form page.

Please note that this is different from the "header and description"

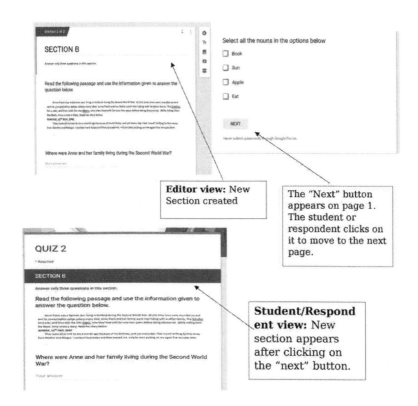

Editor view: New Section created

The "Next" button appears on page 1. The student or respondent clicks on it to move to the next page.

Student/Respondent view: New section appears after clicking on the "next" button.

Question Settings/Options

NOTE: The illustration above explains the different tools you will see constantly around your question, and how to use them. See more below.

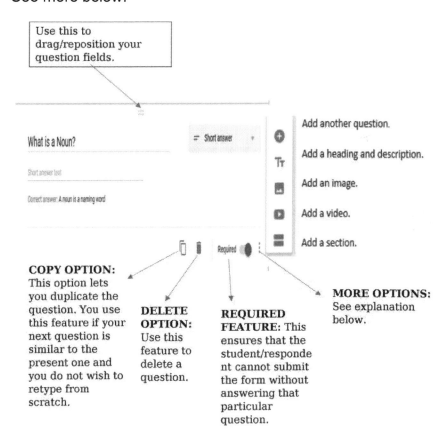

Use this to drag/reposition your question fields.

What is a Noun?

≒ Short answer ▾

Short answer text

Correct answer: A noun is a naming word

Add another question.

Add a heading and description.

Add an image.

Add a video.

Add a section.

Required

COPY OPTION:
This option lets you duplicate the question. You use this feature if your next question is similar to the present one and you do not wish to retype from scratch.

DELETE OPTION:
Use this feature to delete a question.

REQUIRED FEATURE: This ensures that the student/responde nt cannot submit the form without answering that particular question.

MORE OPTIONS:
See explanation below.

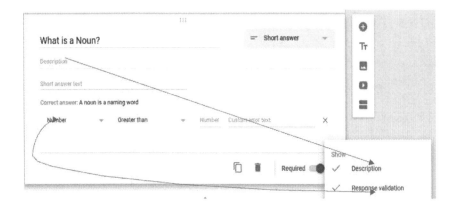

More Options: When you click on the three dots below your question, certain options will pop out (which we can call MORE OPTIONS), depending on the question type. Some of these options appear based on the question type.

For example, under Short Answer and other question types, we have,

1) Description: This can be used when you feel that a brief explanation needs to be given to enable the student or the respondent understand the question asked better. Checking this feature makes the description field appear under the question.

2) Response Validation: This feature ensures that the student/respondent only inputs certain features before he/she can submit the form. The response validation available for now includes;

a) Number: If you want the student to input a value within a certain range. For example, you can ask your students "how many bones do we have in the human body"? The answer is 206. You therefore select a response validation of "number", then choose from the number range options (greater than, less than, etc.), then enter the value depending on range option selected. Custom error text is simply the message the student receives if his/her answer doesn't fall within your selected range.

b) Text: This feature ensures that the student inputs or doesn't input certain characters. Have you ever tried to create a password and you were prompted to use a password with uppercase, lowercase, etc. Yeah! That's it! This has four kinds of validation. i) Contains: When you want the student to input certain text. ii) Doesn't Contain: When you want to ensure that the student doesn't put in certain text. Both "contain" and "doesn't contain" must be specified in the "text" field following it. iii) Email: This ensures that a valid email address (with @ and .com or .xxx) is put in when asking for email addressing. iv) URL: This ensures that a valid website address is put into the answer field.

c) Length: This feature ensures that the student doesn't put in more than the specified number of characters. E.g. when asking for phone numbers, you can set this length to Minimum of 9 (for telephones) or Maximum of 14 for mobile phones with +234.

d) Regular expression: This is almost the same as text but differs because it contains "matches" and "not matches" feature. So, the answer the student gives won't just contain certain words but may or may not match certain words.

Note: Whichever question the above features appear, they mean the same thing.

3) Shuffle Option Order: This feature ensures that every respondent doesn't see each question option in the same order. This is particularly helpful to teachers, as it helps you checkmate cheating amongst your students. This feature will show as "shuffle row order" for multiple or checkbox choice grid.

4) Go to section based on answer: This feature is used when you want the next question to only appear based on the answer of the previous question. So, you can select where each option will take you to if selected, either to a submit button or to a new section or to page 2 of the form (Sections will be explained much later).

Getting Started for Teacher

G oogle Classroom is going to make things much easier for teachers. Many teachers are frustrated by the time wasted in the classroom, passing out papers, grading essays and trying to give feedback. Google Classroom can make this easier in so many ways! Let's explore how Google Classroom is going to transform the way that teachers work so that they can spend more time with the students and less time with all that paperwork!

Setting Up the Classroom

Setting up your classroom is going to be easier than you think. While a lot of other learning platforms ask you to jump through hoops and learn a lot of different tabs before getting to use the system, Google Classroom tries to keep it simple. Some of the things that you need to do to start with Classroom include:

1. Visit classroom.google.com. You will be able to sign up for your account in this part, using your school email address to login. If your school administrator has some special rules about which emails to use, you will need to talk to them.

2.   Click the "+" that is located on the right on top of the page. This allows you to create the first class. Click "Create class."

3.   Name the class so that it is easy to remember. Consider not only the name of the class but also the section. This is important if you are teaching more than one section of the same class. You can say something like Senior English: Period 2. Name the class anything you want, just think about how you will recognize them later.

4.   Now that the class is created, your students can join it. You can send the link to the students in your class to ensure they get into the right section. While waiting for students to join, be a bit creative. Change up the theme to make it match the course name or just to something you like.

5.   Don't forget to fill out the "About" section. This is going to be useful to students before starting your class because it gives them some information about the course. Place information such as your email, the syllabus, grading scale, and other information that the students may need through the year.

Daily Use of Classroom

Once your Classroom is set up and students star to join, it is up to you to have fun with the layout and make the platform work with you. There are some things that you can do with this platform to help students learn including:

- Make announcements—this helps you communicate with the whole class. Simply click on the "Announcement" button and then write the message you want them to do. It is possible to provide links, YouTube videos, and files from your Google Drive to the announcement if needed.

- Add assignments—following the same idea as announcements; you can create a new assignment. Simply write out the name of the assignment, a short description, and attach any files that are necessary. Make sure to add the due date so students can prepare.

- Manage students—to manage your students, go to the "Students" tab. From here, you can allow students to comment, post and comment, or just to read the material. You can send emails to one or two students at a time, and even remove them from the class if they end up switching.

- Grading assignments—after the assignment due date is up, you can click on a student's name to see the files attached. You can then click on "No Grade" and then place the grade that you want to give them. If the system automatically graded a student based on your settings, you can always go back in and change the grade. Make sure to hit "Return" when done to make the changes.

Things Classroom Doesn't Do

Google Classroom has a lot of great features and can make teaching a bit easier, but there are a few things that it is not able to do for teachers. Luckily, with just a bit of work on your part and using the tools that Google provides, it is still possible to finish these tasks and get them to the students without too much hassle. Some of the things that Classroom is not able to do include:

- Provide quizzes and tests—while you can send quizzes and tests as assignments through Classroom, this platform will not create them for you. Using Google Forms, you can create the test and then send a link to your assignments. With the help of Flubaroo, the quizzes are graded for you, but all of this will be outside Google Classroom.

- Chat—as of right now, Classroom does not have a chat feature. You can use other Google Apps to chat or rely on email to communicate.

- Full-featured Forums—the forum feature is not present in this platform, but you can use Forms and Drive to start discussions in your class.

With most of these disadvantages, there are ways to work around them so you can still get all the features you want, you just need to utilize the various apps that Google provides.

What Else Can I do with Google Classroom?

There is so much that you can do with this Google platform! Whether you want to move your whole class online and spend time in class learning and having fun, or you just want to place homework assignments online so students don't misplace them, Google Classroom is the answer you need.

Better Organization

When taking care of twenty or more students, it is easy to become disorganized and misplace things. If you have more than one class, the disorganization can get really bad. Classroom makes this easier by separating each class out, allowing you to set individual due dates, and having your students place their homework all in one place. Some ways that Classroom helps keep teachers organized include:

- The student will be able to place their work in one folder where the teacher can access it from Google Drive. The teacher will then be able to give feedback or show grades in the same place.

- Homework collection is all done in one place. Depending on the assignment, the teacher can even provide feedback while the student is working on it.

- Less time on administrative tasks means the teacher can spend time answering questions and teaching.

- The ability to choose if a document can be edited or only viewed.

- Anytime the teacher needs to post an assignment, question, or announcement; the Classroom will send it to every student. This saves time compared to sending information out to each student.

- The ability to send messages to individual students as well. If you need to notify one or two students about a meeting or homework assignment, it is possible without notifying the whole class.

Organization can be a teachers' best friend. It allows them to think clearly, have more time for students, and get the work done on time. Google Classroom can make staying organized easier than ever.

Work is Easier

Everyone likes it when their work is easier, and Google Classroom can make this happen. It is easy to use; if you already know how to use a few Google apps, you are set for becoming an expert with Classroom. Classroom allows teachers to assess how their students are doing, connect with the whole class or individual students and even monitor how students are doing all while attending other work. Some of the great things that you can do with Classroom to make your work easier include:

- Teachers in the same district can be on different domains while still sharing content and files together. If you know, a teacher in the district that has a workbook you like or you both want to connect your students together; this can happen through Classroom.

- The reuse feature allows you to reuse any of the information that you have used before including questions, assignments, and announcements. For example, if you teach the same class again the second semester, you use have the reuse feature to place assignments back up.

- Classroom is easy to set up. Once your district signs up, you just need to use your assigned email and set up the classes that you want. Prepare everything that is needed in one area to share with your students.

- Everything is paperless. No more handing out papers, standing in line for the copy machine, or worrying about students losing assignments. Everyone in your class can log on and get to work.

- Classroom is very accessible, available through tablets, PC's, laptops, and now even on some smartphones.

- If you are planning on going on vacation, you can plan it all out ahead of time, scheduling assignments and other announcements before you leave. The platform will send you an email when the posts go live, and your substitutes can stay on schedule even when you're not there.

Grading Process

Grading papers, assignments, and tests can take hours of a teachers' time. The more classes you take on, the longer the grading process can take. While teachers want to give each student the attention they deserve, they also have to prepare for classes and keep up with home life as well. Classroom can help to make the grading process easier, helping students to get faster results and freeing up time for the teacher. Classroom can help by:

- Making it easier to grade. The teacher will be able to pull up a spreadsheet and add in the grades as well as any feedback. Once you press the "Return" button, the students will be able to see their grades.

- Making it easier to monitor students once they have completed assignments. The teacher can also give feedback and grade them right away.

- Making it easy to see who has and hasn't turned in their assignments.

- Offering options for grading students. They can choose from a numerical value already in the system or create their value. Students will be able to see the grades once they are imported.

- Allowing for instant grading. There are add-ons to the program that allow for instant grading. For worksheets and multiple choice options, these add-ons can take care of the grading and free up time.

Communication

There are many times when teachers and students will need to communicate, and Classroom can make this easier than ever. Teachers will be able to make announcements, send out assignments, and provide feedback to the students. And students will have the opportunity to ask questions when needed. Some of the things you can do with Classroom for open communication include:

- Opening up a question and answer portion. This allows for more discussion both inside and outside the class.

- Teachers can use a "Create a Question" feature to start the discussion. Use this for polls and surveys to see how well the students understand the topic.

- Post topics and questions to start an online discussion. This can be used during class for small group discussions or for homework to get students thinking and communicating about the reading.

- Emailing can help with asking questions, sending reminders (especially during long breaks), and getting other information out to students.

- Discussions can help students to understand the material more and opens up students who may be shy and less likely to discuss during class.

Becoming More Creative

Sometimes, your classroom will need a bit more creativity to get the point across. While math topics may be fine with just adding worksheets and tests on Classroom, others like English and Science can allow for some more creativity. Classroom makes it easier to change things up to facilitate different learning styles to make education more fun. Some of the things you can do to change up learning through in Classroom include:

- Work on discussions. This can help everyone participate in class, even those who may be too shy in class to speak up.

- Multi-media is easy to use in Classroom. Bring in YouTube videos, pictures from online, or anything else that can supplement your lessons.

- Create your games. Have students compete to answer questions, create your own learning board game, or find some great options online to fit your topics.

- Offer different project options. While some people may like to create a poster or write an essay, others may be better at performances, speaking, or singing. These can all be done and uploaded on Classroom as well.

Creativity makes the classroom so much better and can allow for more learning than you will find with just using a textbook. Google Classroom allows you to try out different types of learning materials without adding to your workload.

Classroom is one of the best tools that teachers can use to make life easier. Rather than spending so much time on administrative tasks like making copies, finding new tests, and grading, Classroom allows everything to be in one place. Add in the benefits of using different learning materials, and Classroom will change the way students learn.

Getting Started for Student

As a student, you are going to be impressed by all of the things that you are able to do with the help of Google Classroom. While teachers are going to be able to assign homework and invite you to the classroom, there are a lot of benefits that you will be able to get when you decide to use Google Classroom as well. The benefits are not just there for the teachers as students will like all of the options that are there for them to learn as well. This chapter is going to go over some of the things that students should know about using Google Classroom and getting it to work for them.

In this chapter, you will be able to take a look at how to get onto your own personal Google Classroom Account and how to set it up so that you are able to get into the classes that you will like. You are going to have just one Google Classroom Account to get on to all of your classes in one place. You can even see that your assignments are all going to be collected in one place because they will all connect to the same Calendar. When you are done with this chapter, you will be able to get into your account, sign up for your classes, and so much more with the help of Google Classroom.

Signing In

The first thing that you need to know how to do is how to sign in. If you aren't able to get onto the Google Classroom, it is going to be really hard to see which classes are available for you to do, submit assignments, work with some of the other students on some of your projects, or use the other neat features that are available with Google Classroom. Some of the steps that you need in order to sign into Google Classroom includes:

With a Web Browser

To log in with a web browser, you would first need to visit classroom.google.com and then click on the student tab.

Type in the credentials that your teacher has set up for you or the ones that you have from your own accounts.

From here you will be able to go on a guided tour of the virtual classroom and learn how to use all of the neat tools that are there.

With an Android or iOS App

If you want to sign into Google Classroom with the help of a mobile app, this is possible, you would just need to go through and use the following steps to make it happen:

- Touch the icon that looks like a person.

- Now enter in all of the details that you have for your Google Apps for Education and then continue with signing in.

- Select Student before touching on submit.

- At this point, you will have a choice to either take a guided tour of the classroom or not. If you decide not to take this tour, you can click on Skip to miss out on it.

As you can see, you will find that it is pretty easy to join a class inside of Google Classroom. In most cases, you will just need to wait to get an invitation from your teacher for the class, which your teacher will be able to send out simply by having your email address. In some cases, the teacher will give you a code and you will be able to place that into the code box once you are signed into classroom.google.com. Both methods are easy to use and will ensure that you are getting into the right classes that you need in order to get all of your work done and to use all of the cool resources that your teacher has set up.

Viewing the Class Resource Page

Once you are added to a classroom, it is time to know what is going on in your particular class. You will want to have a good idea what this particular class is about and some of the resources that the teacher has made available for you to use.

In order to view the resource page for your class, you would go through the following steps:

- Click on the class that you have joined If you are in more than one class, make sure that you are in the right one.

- From here, you will click on About and then choose the item that you would like to take a look at.

Depending on the class that you are working with, there may be a few different things that will show up inside of this part so look around and see what is available. This is a great way to become familiar with the class that you are working in and to make sure that you are able to find what you need later on.

Viewing an Archived Class

After you have finished with a class, such as when a class is over at the end of a semester or the school year, you are able to archive that class. This moves it out of the way but still has it around so you can see things that are in it for later on. If you find out later on that you need some of the information from a class or you would like to review some of the resources that were in that class after it has ended, you are able to check out your archived classes if you would like. In order to view these Archived Classes, you can do the following steps:

1.   Click on your Menu and then select the button that says All Archived Classes.

2.   Select the class that you would like to look at.

From here, you will be able to go through this class and get whatever information that you would like. You can look at some of the resources, the various projects you worked on and more. You will need to make sure that you archive all of your classes when they end so that you can get this information later on. You never know when you will need to get this information again so always be careful before deleting or doing other things to some of your old classes when you get done with them.

Any time that you would like to go through and see some of your own projects or some of the information that is in your other classes, such as when you would like to review an easier class before going into a more advanced class, you can use the steps above. The archived classes will stick around so that you are able to watch what is going on and get the information that you would like from each one whenever you need.

Viewing the Class Calendar

There are many times when you may need to take a look at the class calendar. This will let you know what assignments are coming up in the class when big tests will happen, and the other big events that the teacher adds into it. This can really be helpful for you to keep everything in one place and you won't have to always remember the dates all of the time. It is a great way to help you have an idea of what you should expect in class and what you are expected to do. In order to view your class calendar, you will need to use the following steps:

- Click on the Calendar button when you are in your Classroom Page.

- From here you can click on an assignment inside of the Calendar if you would like to know about a specific assignment, or you can click on Quick Question to have access to this information from your Student page.

- Then you can click on the arrow to have an idea of what is going on over the next week or more based on what information you need.

- If you would like to filter the events so that you can see something in particular. Lick on All Classes and then choose the class that you feel like filtering events for.

- This will then show you the information that you want to take a look at.

And that is all that you will need to do in order to look at some of the assignments that are coming due for your class. You can switch around between classes and look at the due dates for the various assignments that you need to get done with. This is a good way to take a look at due dates, tests, and other important dates that your teacher posts all in one location.

Setting Up Your Mobile Notifications

One of the options that you are able to work with is to set up some mobile notifications about your classes. This can be really helpful because it allows you to know right away when a new assignment or a new announcement is posted by your teacher. It can also show you when someone mentions you in a post or a discussion so that you can give an answer back. In some cases, it is going to help you to send and receive some private notes, correspond with others in your classroom, and will even provide you with a way to get your ratings and grades for assignments right away.

There are several different methods that you can use in order to set up these mobile notifications. To set these up for your iOS, you would need to use the following steps:

1. Touch the icon that looks like a person before touching on Settings, Notifications, and then Notifications again.

2. Choose to Allow Notifications at this point and then you can choose whether you want those notifications to be turned off or if you would like to turn them on.

3.   If you want to see how many notifications you have, you can then go in and choose Show inside the Notification Center.

4.   If you would like to have a certain sound come up when you receive a notification on your iOS device, you can turn on sounds at this time.

5.   You can even go through and make it so that the notifications will show up even if you happen to have your screen locked. You just need to click on Show Notifications on Lockscreen to make this happen.

There are a few other alert types that you are able to choose from when working with this step on your iOS. You can choose to work with alerts, which will show your notifications right in the center of the screen. If you click on banners here you will see your notifications show up right on the top of the screen. If you click on none, you will need to swipe down so that you can see what notifications are there for you.

If you would like to be able to set up your notifications on your Android device, you would need to use the following steps to make it happen:

1.   Here you will want to touch on the icon that looks like a person.

2. From here you can scroll down until you reach your settings, and make sure that you check on the vibration and the sounds if you would like to have these while you get your notifications.

3. Any time that you would like to turn off these notifications with your Android device, you just need to go back in and click the right buttons to make this happen.

Getting notifications sent to your phone is pretty simple and can help you to have a good idea of what is going on in each of your classes. If you like to stay on top of your classes and you like to know ahead of time when a new test or project is due even if you are out and doing other things, setting up the notifications on your iOS or Android device can be pretty easy to accomplish. You are able to see these notifications when you log in to your student account, but in some cases, it is easier to have all of these notifications sent directly to your phone.

How to change your account settings

If you have a Google Classroom Account, it is possible to go through and change the settings so that it works the way that you would like. Sometimes you may only want to change one or two things about your account, and other times you will want to change quite a bit so that the account works the way that you would like. If you want to change the settings on your Google Classroom Account, this can be pretty simple to work on. You just need to go to the Classroom Page before selecting Settings. From here you are able to change any of the settings that you would like for that classroom. Some of the things that you are able to change in here include:

- See when someone tags you in a post or if they send you a comment.

- When there are some new assignments, or if the teacher has sent an assignment back to you.

- Whenever a teacher gives you a new grade for that classroom.

- Whenever someone sends you a private comment or message so that you are able to respond.

- Whenever a teacher posts out a new announcement or assignment for the classroom.

As you can see, there are many different things that you are able to do when you work with your own Google Classroom. This chapter spent some time helping you to get started with setting up your account and getting organized so that you can start to get the most out of your classes. After you are done with this chapter, you are all set to start getting the most out of all the great features that are available with your Google Classroom.

Tips for Differentiation and Tools to Use

Both teachers and students can benefit from Google Classroom. It is an easy platform that brings together some of the best apps that Google has to offer to help teachers get the most out of their lectures and students to learn in new and exciting ways. Here we will look at some of the tips and tricks that both students and teachers can try to get the most out of the Google Classroom platform.

Tips for Teachers

Tip 1: Learn all the ways to give feedback.

Your students are going to thrive with as much feedback as you can provide them and Classroom offers you many options for this. You can leave comments on assignments that students hand in, on the file that is submitted, through email, and so much more. Consider the best places to leave feedback and let your students know so they can be on the lookout for ways to improve.

Some of the ways that you can utilize comments include:

- Class comments—you can do this by starting a common for the whole class on the outside of the assignment or in the announcement. This is going to be a comment that the whole class is going to see so don't use it if you just want to talk to the individual student. It is a good option to use if you want to answer a question that a lot of people have.

- Private comments—you can do this by going into the file of an individual student. You will be able to see the submissions this student has made and can click on the comment bar near the bottom. When you add a comment, the student will be the only one who can see it.

- Comments to media—you can do this by clicking on the file that the student submitted to you. Highlight the area and then comment on that particular part of the project. This can help you to show an example of the student or explain your thoughts and how something needs to be changed.

Tip 2: Use the description feature

When creating an assignment, make sure to add a nice long description. This is where you explain what the assignment is all about, how to complete it, and even when the assignment is due. Often students are juggling many classes all at once and by the time they get to the assignment, they have forgotten all the instructions you gave them in class. Or if a student missed class that day, the description can help them understand what they missed. A good description can help to limit emails with questions and can help students get started on the assignment without confusion.

Tip 3: Use Flubaroo

Grading can take up a lot of your time, especially when dealing with many students and multiple classes. You want to provide your students with accurate feedback as quickly as possible, but traditional teaching can make this impossible. Add-ons like Flubaroo can make this easier. When creating a quiz or test, you can use Flubaroo so that when a student submits their answers, the app will check them and provide a score right away. The student can see how well they did on the quiz and where they may need to make some changes.

This kind of add-on is best for things such as multiple choice assignments and tests. It allows the student to see what they understand right away without having to wait for the teacher to correct everything. You are able to go back and change the grade on a particular assignment if the add-on grades incorrectly, you want to add bonus points, or for some other reason.

If you are creating assignments like discussion posts, opinions, projects, and essays, Flubaroo is not the best option for you.

This app is not going to understand how to grade these projects and since each one is more creative and doesn't necessarily have a right or wrong answer, it is important for the teacher to go in and grade. There are many places where you can provide feedback, even at various points of the project, to help the student make changes before the final grade.

Tip 4: Reuse some of your old posts

At times, you may have an assignment, question, or announcement that is similar to something you have posted before. For example, if you have a weekly reading or discussion assignment that is pretty much the same every week, you will be able to use the reuse option on Classroom. To do this, just click on the "+" button that is on the bottom right of the screen. You will then be able to select "Reuse post." Pick from a list of options that you already used for the class. If there are any modifications, such as a different due date, you can make those before posting again. When reusing the post, you have the option to create new copies of the attachments that were used in the original posting.

Tip 5: Share your links and resources

There may be times that you find an interesting document, video, or other media that you would like your students to see. Or they may need resources for an upcoming project, and you want to make it easier for them to find. In this case, you should use the announcement feature. This allows all the important documents to be listed right at the top of the classroom rather than potentially getting lost further down in assignments.

This is a great tip to use for items of interest that you would like to share with your students or for documents and files that they will need right away. If you have a resource that the students will need throughout the year, you should place it into the "About" tab to prevent it getting lost as the year goes on.

Tips for Students

Tip 1: Pick one email for all of your classes

Consider having a dedicated email that is for all of your classes. You don't need to separate it and have an email for each of your classes, but create a new email that will only accept information from all classes using Google Classroom. Whenever a teacher announces they use this platform, you will use this email. This helps you to keep all of your classes in one place and can prevent you from missing out on your announcements and assignments because they got lost in all your personal emails.

Tip 2: Check your classes daily

As the year goes on, your teacher will probably get into a routine of when they make posts, and you can check the class at that time. But it is still a good idea to stay on top of a class and check it each day. You never know when you may forget about an assignment that is almost due or when the teacher will add an extra announcement for the whole class. If you only check your classes on occasion, you could miss out on a lot of important information along the way. Check in daily to stay up to date and to get everything in on time.

Tip 3: Look at the calendar

One of the first places you should go when opening up to a class is the Calendar. This is going to list everything important that is coming your way in the next few months (updated as the teacher adds new announcements and assignments) so you can plan out your time. For some students, it is easier to get a grasp on the work when it is in table form rather than just looking at a date in the announcements. Use this as a planning tool and check it often to see if there is anything new to add to your schedule.

Tip 4: Ask questions for clarification

Classroom makes it easier for students to ask the questions they need before starting an assignment. In some classrooms, it can be hard to find time to ask a question. When twenty or more students are asking questions at the same time, or the teacher runs out of time and barely gets the assignment out before the next bell, there are many students who may leave the classroom without any clue how to begin on an assignment.

With Classroom, the students can ask any questions they have when it is convenient. If they have a question about an assignment, they can comment on the assignment or send an email. If they have a question about some feedback that is left for a test, discussion, or essay, they can ask it right on the assignment. Classroom has opened up many options for talking to your teacher and getting your questions answered so don't be shy and sit in the dark when you need clarification.

Tip 5: Learn about all the features of Google

Google has many great features that both students and teachers can take advantage of. Many people don't realize all of the different apps that are available on Google, and since these apps can be used together with Classroom and are free, it is important to take advantage of as many as possible. Some of the best Google products that can help with learning include:

- Gmail—Gmail makes it easier for students and teachers to communicate about the class without sharing the information with other students.

- Calendar—students will be able to see at a glance when important assignments, tests, and other information occurs in their class.

- Drive—Drive is a great place to put all assignments, questions, and other documents that are needed to keep up in class. Teachers can place learning materials and assignments inside for the student to see and students can submit their assignments all in one place.

- YouTube—students are used to spending time on YouTube, and teachers can use this to their advantage to find educational videos for their class. Students can either look at links that the teacher provides or search for their videos.

- Docs—this program works similar to Microsoft Word, but since it is free, it can be nice for those students who don't already have Word at home. Students can write, edit, and make changes just like on regular documents and then submit back to the teacher.

- Google Earth/Maps—explore the world around us with these two great features. Google Earth lets students learn more about the world by allowing them to look up different areas and see them from an actual satellite. Google Maps can help with Geography around the world or students can even create their Maps with this program.

These are just a few of the different apps available with Google that can make a difference in the way that students learn. While not all of them will apply to every class, a good understanding of each can help the teacher pick the right one for their class and helps the student learn as much as possible.

Tip 6: Don't forget about tests and quizzes

Sometimes, a teacher may give you a few days to complete a test at home if there isn't enough time to do everything in the classroom. This gives you a bit of freedom to study for longer and fit the test around your schedule, but when a test isn't due right away, it is sometimes easy to forget about it. Make sure to watch your Calendar and set up announcements to remind yourself that an important assignment or test is due.

The issue with forgetting about some of these things is that with the right add-ons, the system may grade the test as incomplete or give you a zero (if the test is multiple choice). The teacher may be willing to go back in and fix the grade or extend the due date if you talk to them, but it is still better to just get the test done in the first place. This shows that you can adhere to deadlines and saves some time for your teacher.

Google Classroom may seem like a simple platform, but there is just so much that you can do with it both as a teacher and as a student. The options for learning, sending information back and forth, and all the organization and freedom now available in the classroom can make this an attractive choice for many schools.

Demonstrations of Learning

Teaching Math

I f you are thinking how else you can expand the experience of learning math or using Classroom in your math classes, here are some creative ways to build on.

1. Problem of the Week

Aptly known as POW, POWs can be anything that you feel needs more attention. It can be a problem you have identified or a problem that your students can identify. You can create games that can help students learn about the problem differently and participating students can submit their work directly to Google Classroom.

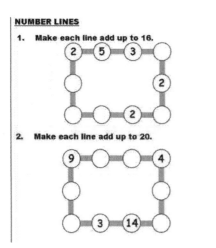

2. Link Interactive Simulations

There are several websites dedicated to providing helpful math simulations. Sites like Explore Learning have thousands of math simulations and math variations that students can look up to solve mathematical problems. You can link these URLs in your classroom either as part of an assignment or through an Announcement.

3. Link to Playsheets

Playsheets fall between gamification and GBL. Teachers can link up relevant Playsheets and give these are assignment for students. These playsheets give immediate feedback to students and it is an excellent learning and motivational tool that tells the students that they are on the right track.

4. Use Google Draw

Google Draw is another creative tool that allow students and teachers to create virtual manipulations such as charts, Algebra tiles and so on. Draw images that make it easy for students to identify with Math. This can be used to create differentiated assignments targeting students with different learning levels.

5. Use digital tools

Digital tools can also be used to solve various math problems. These tools can be used from Google Drive and integrated with other Google documents. Once done, students can submit their solved problems to Google Classroom.

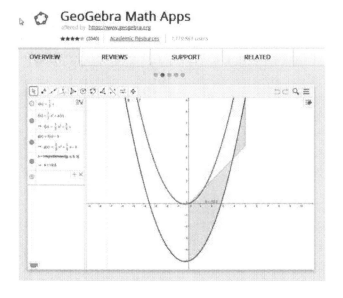

Teach Programming

Get students to use programs that can enable them to exhibit their understanding of mathematical concepts.

Teaching Science

1. Hangout with Experts

Get an expert you are connected to in real life to talk about their experiences either working in a science related field or to help students with science related subjects. You can use Google Hangouts to send questions the class has and link it to your Google Classroom. This enables the students to access the Hangout and participate in the questioning or even watch the interview after the session is done. The Hangout Session can be archived for later viewing.

2. Collecting Evidence

Have your students submit 'evidence' of science experiments by sending it photos or videos of their science projects and upload it to Google Classroom.

3. Give Real life examples

Tailor-make your science projects and assignments so that it gets students going out to get real life samples which they can record on their mobile devices. They can take these images and submit it immediately to the Google Classroom. Make it interesting- students that submit their answers faster get extra points!

4. Crowdsourcing information

Get students into the whole idea and activity of crowdsourcing. Create a Google Spreadsheet with a specific topic and specify what information they need and what goals the project needs to accomplish. Upload the document to Google Classroom and get students to find and contribute information.

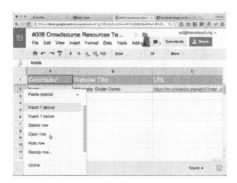

Teaching Writing & Reading

1. Provide Templates

Allow students to access writing templates on Google Classroom for things such as formal letters, informal letters, report writing, assignment templates, resumes and cover letter formats.

2. Reading Records

Establish a weekly reading record on Google Classroom where they can record information on the times that they have read during the week. So instead of writing it down on a reading diary, allow them to update a form on Google Classroom by entering the necessary data. This allows them to immediately add in the information of the books that they have read while it is still fresh in their minds.

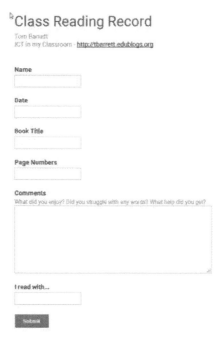

3. Collaborate on Writing Projects

Get your students to collaborate on writing projects via Group assignments. These projects can be anything from preparing newspaper articles, journals, e-portfolios and so on.

4. Spelling Tests

You can create a simple 1-10 or 1-20 weekly spelling test via Google Form. Get students to type in their answers as you read out the list of words. Once completed, apply formula to judge if they are correct or not and it becomes self-marking.

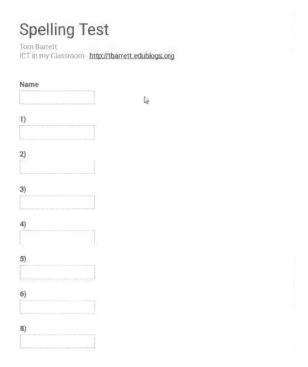

Teaching Physical Education

Didn't think PE could be done via Google Classroom? Here are some ideas:

1. Post Fitness Videos

Post fitness videos to help your students understand how to perform a workout. Send out videos to any psychical activity that you want students to conduct on their next PE session or you can also just post a video after classes so students can practice the exercise in their own time and work on their form.

2. Get students to post videos of their daily workout

Have your students post videos in the public feed on your Google Classroom with a hashtag such as #midweekfitspo. Encourage students to work out and post their videos each week.

3. Link to safety videos

Post up safety videos for your PE activities so your students know what kind of skills that they need to follow in order to exercise safely.

4. Post Resources for activities

PE teachers can also post up useful resources for games and activities such as rules and method of playing ahead in time before the student's next PE session. It would help the students prepare and know what to expect for their next class.

5. Create a Fitness Tracker

Assign students to a Fitness Tracker spreadsheet and make a copy for each student. Assign a due date for the end of the semester for their physical education class. You can monitor each student's progress by checking out the assignment folder in the Google Classroom.

Use the spreadsheet to get your students to track their progress. Whenever students update their results, the spreadsheet automatically updates to dynamic charts so students can see their progress visually over the entire semester.

You can either pair students up to work in partners or individually. Get the students take photos of each other's forms when practicing certain tasks so that you can evaluate their form and correct it by way of giving them feedback via Classroom or during PE classes. A rubric would be helpful here too so that students can self-evaluate their own workouts and make corrections where necessary.

Other Teaching Methods to Use

1. Attach Patterns and Structures

Upload patterns and structures that students and identify and explain. Students can also collaborate with other student to identify patterns and structures to come up with solutions.

2. Use geometric concepts

Use Google Drawings or Slides to insert drawings of geometric figures for maths, science and even for art.

3. Collaborate online with other teachers

If you know other teachers have modules or projects which would come in handy with your class, collaborate together and enable your students to join is as well. Different teachers allow for different resources and the teaching load can also be distributed.

4. Peer Tutoring

Senior students can also be allowed to access your Google Classroom at an agreed time on a weekly basis to tutor and give support to junior students or students in differentiated assignments.

5. Celebrate success

Google Classroom also enables the teacher to encourage students through comments whenever they submit and assignment because feedback can be given immediately and this can be done either private or publicly

6. Digital quizzes

Quizzes can be used for various subjects on Google Classroom. Get your students to submit their answers quickly for extra points.

7. Share presentations

Share whatever presentations and slides that you have with your students to help them with whatever assignments that you have given them.

Things You Can Do with Google Classroom

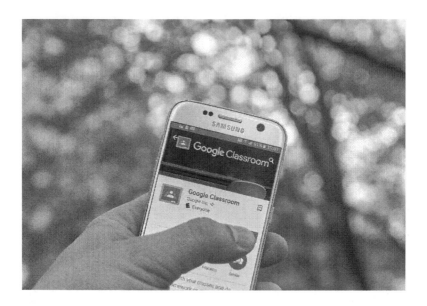

So, what can you do with Google Classroom? Well, there is a lot, and here, we will highlight just what you can do with this in order to achieve the best results possible with this service.

Sharing content with the class

If you're a teacher or student, you will want to know what you can do with the messages you need to communicate. You will see when you open it up the stream tab, and from there, you can click the box that says share with the class so you can share it with the entire class. You can from there attach various files, videos from YouTube, and external links that come with the message. This is perfect for teachers if you feel like you want to give the class an extra resource for learning, so that it can facilitate that, and make it easier for you to utilize and do as well. You can pose questions with this too, which is great for students if they need to ask something, or would like to begin a discussion with the class.

For teachers as well, you can also make announcements here too, so if you decide to change the due date on something, you do not have to worry about a student "not hearing or paying attention to it" since it is definitely much easier for you to get the announcement directly out to the class.

Assignment Fun

For teachers, this will be your new best friend. While you can share resources, in the assignments tab, you can actually create lessons. In addition, assignments for the student to look at. Just press the plus sign, and you will then be given the option to create a new full-fledged assignment for them to utilize.

All of these assignments have due dates as well, and you can from there, click on the "to-do" list I order to see what you need to complete, and from there, you can press the dun button in order to make sure that you get the assignment in within the time period

teachers can also tag these assignments by topic, which is a lifesaver, and many times, you can when you're choosing to create a post, you can literally lick on the topic button, giving you a chance to add the topics based on the section. So, if you want to create assignments and the like based on chapter units, topics, or the type of assignment, you'll have that extra tag, and it can definitely help with organizing this, and it helps students too, so that they can find the assignment immediately when needed.

At this point, students can go to their assignments, open it to do this, and from there, if you cannot do something, or your'e confused, comment on it. I there is an attachment, you can download this to the drive, do this, and from there, turn it in. turning in assignments has never been easier, because students do not' need to worry about potentially losing it, which is super nice, and it makes the whole struggle of assignments easier.

Creating Quizzes and Assignments

If you are a teacher who is looking for a more paperless means of content creation, then you should definitely consider Google Classroom. You can from there, put together Google forms, attaching it to an assignment tab, and from there, you can edit the quiz and the questions as well. If you have an assignment you want to reuse, you can do so, that is the beauty of this, and you can crate assignments, and reuse them, so you do not have to make it again. You can also add feedback, various point values, and also release their grades as they turn them in, and from there, you can pretty much take everything online, saving a lot of paper in the process. This is probably one of the best parts of Google Classroom, since there is a lot that you can do here, and a lot, that children can utilize over time.

Manage Different Classes

If you are a teacher that manages different classes, this will make classroom management so much easier, that in turn will help with learning, and you do not need to worry so much about juggling the lesson plans for each class. You can re-use the existing assignments and questions that you tried in another class, and you can also share posts and announcements with so many different classes, which makes it so much easier, and if you have references that you want to use, you can always archive them, so that next year you can go in, get the same posts, and then use them with the same class as well.

But what, there's even more, if you have a co-teacher, you can have them sign in and help you out with this, and you can invite another teacher that can help you with the learning aspects of the classroom. This is super great, since you do not have to spend as much time trying to put together lesson plans, and if you have multiple teachers helping, it can make everything a lot easier.

Creating Resources Page

Finally, you can create class resources pages. This is awesome for those teachers that have to deal with many of the different issues that come from trying to get all of their students the information that they need. This resources page has everything all in the right place, so if they need extra info, especially video and other learning resources information, then this is the perfect thing for them, and it can make it much easier for teachers too.

With Google Classroom, everything is made easier, and you can get the full benefits of what you can use, and in turn, help out more students than ever before.

Guidelines & Suggestions for Classroom Management and Instructional Forms

Google Classroom allows you to extend the blended learning experience in a variety of ways and come 2017; teachers can create excellent number of ways to enhance a student's grasp of school subjects and increase learning capabilities. The possibilities are endless where Google is concerned.

Google's biggest asset is its simplicity and ease of use. Using the various Google applications doesn't require a textbook to learn it, as with Google Classroom, all other apps are simple to set up, quick to learn and saves time and energy to get things done and organize your various files and documents. In this chapter, we will share ten best practices for Google Classroom that you can employ, to fully make use and take advantage of this pioneering online education tool.

1. Reduce the carbon footprints of your class

The idea of Google Classroom is to make things easier for teachers and students alike when learning things. It takes the conventional classroom and places it on the online sphere and enables students and educators to create spreadsheets and presentations, online documents and it makes sharing and communicating easier. Creating and sharing things digitally eliminates the need to printing. Schools use a lot of papers but utilizing Classroom enables you to remove the necessity of paper for simple things. Have an assignment? Save some trees, time and money by creating them on Classroom, distributing it to your students in your Classroom.

2. Distribute and Collect Student's homework easily

The whole point of creating the assignments via Google Classroom is so that you can distribute it and collect the assignments quickly. Yes, you can say that you could get it done via email too. But Classroom's enable all these things to be done in one place. You'll know who has sent an assignment, who have passed their deadline and who needs more help with their work. It's all about lessening the hassle in your life.

3. Utilizing the feedback function

With instant access, teachers are able to clarify doubts, concerns and misconceptions their students may have by providing feedback as and when students need it. As teachers, you eliminate possible issues that might arise while students are doing their assignments. This reduces the headache you might have upon receiving the assignments that don't meet the requirements. Assignments that are handed in that have issues can be immediately rectified as well, through private one-on-one feedback with the relevant student.

4. Create your personalized learning environment

The main benefit of Google Classroom is the freedom that it gives teachers. Very often, teachers are required to follow the national syllabus forwarded by the Department or Ministry of Education in a country. While this is rightly done for the sake of uniformity and to ensure students across the country have access to the same level of education, utilizing Classroom, on the other hand, gives teachers the freedom to add and create a different environment for learning.

Teachers can focus on using different materials, subjects, and cater to the different levels and needs of students. If you are using Google Classroom, then make sure you use this aspect to your fullest advantage. You would be able to endorse a personalized learning system by giving your students different learning preferences such as choices of submitting answers, various types of online assignments and using online resources.

5. Encourage real world applications

Encourage students to submit their assignments using real world material whether it's a series of videos or photos, a compilation of multimedia applications, using the many different apps out there to create amazing online presentations are just some of the things that students can do that will increase their learning tendencies and spark online discussions within the Classroom. This enables the students to apply and implement assignments that they have done in their real lives.

6. Allow shy students to participate

As teachers, we know which students are more extrovert that the other. Sometimes in conventional classroom settings, the shy kid or the kid with self-esteem issues or those that lack confidence have problems participating in classroom activities, speaking out or even raising their hand to answer questions. Google Classroom gives a safety barrier for students that fall into this category but allowing them to be more open with discussing and expressing themselves. As the teacher, you can also find creative ways to encourage these students to open up via game-based learning to promote trust, openness, teamwork, and collaboration.

7. Allow for coaching

Some students need more coaching and a little bit more explanation. If you know some students in your class that needs it, you can give them extra instructions by privately messaging them. You can always follow up with them while they are doing their assignments just to check if they are on the right track. Additionally, you can also invite another teacher to collaborate and help with coaching your students.

8. Interactive Activities Using Google Classroom

The more and more you use Google Classrooms, the more you will be able to use Classrooms in many more ways than just connecting with your students and creating assignments.

Google Classroom, combined with other Google products such as Google Slides can really deliver powerful interactive user experiences and deliver engaging and valuable content.

Teachers looking to create engaging experiences in Google Classroom can use Google Slides and other tools in the Google suite of products to create unique experiences.

Here are some exciting ways that you can use Google Classroom and Google Slides to create an engaging learning experience for your students:

1.   Create eBooks via PDF

PDF files are so versatile and you can open them in any kind of device. Want to distribute information only for read-only purposes? Create a PDF! You can use Google Docs or even Google Slides for this purpose and then save it as a PDF document before sending it out to your classroom.

2.   Create a slide deck book

Make your textbooks paperless too, not just assignments. Teachers can derive engaging and interactive content from the web and include it in the slide deck books, upload it to the Google Classroom and allow your students to access them. Make sure to keep it as read only.

3.   Play Jeopardy

This method has been used in plenty of Google Classroom and the idea was created by Eric Curts, a Google Certified Innovator, created this template that you can copy into your own Google Drive to customize with your own questions and answers. Scores can be kept on another slide that only you can control.

4.   Create Game-Show Style Review Games

Another creative teacher came up with a Google Slide of 'Who Wants to be a Millionaire?'. The template allows you to add in your questions and get students to enter the answers in the text box. Again, you keep the score!

5.   Use Animation

Did you know you can create animations in your Google Slide and share in on Classroom? This tutorial shows you how. You can also encourage your students to create animation to explain their assignments. This is really making them push boundaries and think out of the box.

6.   Create stories sand adventures

Using Google Slides and uploading them to Google Classroom to tell a story. Turn a question into a story and teach your students to create an adventure to describe their decision for the outcome of the character in their story. The stories can be a certain path that the students have chosen for the character or a story that explains the process of finding a solution.

7.   Using Flash Cards

Flash cards are great ways to increase the ability to understand a subject or topic. Do you want to create an interactive sessions on Google Classroom using flash cards? You can start by utilizing Google Sheets which gives you a graphic display of words and questions and then to reveal the answers, all you need to do is click. Compared to paper flash cards, these digital flash cards allow you to easily change the questions, colors as well as the answers of the cards depending on what you are teaching the class. Digital flash cards also are an interactive presentation method that is guaranteed to engage your Classroom and bring about a new way of teaching using Google Classroom's digital space.

Make vocabulary lessons, geography lessons and even history lessons fund and entertaining with digital flash cards.

8.   Host an online viewing party

Get your students to connect to Classroom at a pre-determined date and time when there is a noteworthy performance, play or even movie that is related to the subjects you are teaching in your class. Let them view the video together and also interact with them by adding questions to your Google Classroom and allowing your students to reply to you in real time. This way, you can see assess them on their reflections, level of understanding and their observations. You can also give your own interpretation of the scene and explain it again to students who do not quite understand.

There is no limit to what a teacher can do with Google Classroom and the entire Google suite of apps whether its Google Slides or Google Calendar or even Google Maps. The only thing you would need is creativity and the desire to give your student a different experience when using Google Classroom.

Example of Google Form Uses

Uses for Google Forms in the Classroom

CLASSROOM MANAGEMENT & DAY-TO-DAY ACTIVITIES	LESSONS, ASSESSMENT & REFLECTION
Sign-up Sheets	Interest Surveys
Class Information Management	Learner Self-Monitoring Reports
Nomination Forms	Reading Journals
Make-up Request Form for Parents	Learning Logs
Teacher/Colleague Observation	Quizzes & Tests
Attendance Check-ins	Writing Prompts
Annotated Bibliography Collection	Observation Rubrics

Assignment Submitting (Link)	Instant Feedback on Lessons or Instruction
Snack Sign-up Forms	Student-to-Student Data Collection Projects
Scheduling Parent-Teacher Conference	Data Collection for Experiments
Volunteer Sign-up	Peer Feedback
Department & School-wide Surveys	K-W-L for Assessing Prior Knowledge
Technology Issues Reporting Tool	Reading Record
Getting to Know You Class Survey	Project Progress Form
Dialoging with Parents	Observation Tools (checklists; anecdotal notes, etc.)
Placing Orders for Fundraisers	Questioning

Parental Feedback	Beginning-of-Year Technology Skills Survey
Discipline Referrals	Student-Created Choose Your Own Adventure Stories
Creating Lesson Plans	Debate Social Attitudes Form
Manage Classroom Lending Libraries	Website Evaluation Form
Parental Absence Notice	Student Note-Taking
Topic Sign-up Sheets	Global Collaboration
Computer Lab Reservation Form	Exit Tickets
Grading/Observation Rubric	Reservations for Class Trips

Example of Google Form Uses

Parent-Teacher Conference Request

Independent Reading Guide

Rubric (Divided into Two Sections)

Public Speaking Rubric

* Required

The speaker made eye contact with the audience. *
Please rate the speaker's performance using the scale below.

	1	2	3	4	5	6	7	
Did Not Make Eye Contact	○	○	○	○	○	○	○	Made Eye Contact Throughout the Presentation

Rubric for Public Speaking
Please rate each speaker on his/her performance in each area.

	Excellent	Average	Fair	Poor
States the purpose.	○	○	○	○
Organizes the content.	○	○	○	○
Supports ideas.	○	○	○	○
Incorporates stories and examples.	○	○	○	○
Summarizes the main idea(s).	○	○	○	○

NEXT   Page 1 of 2

This content is neither created nor endorsed by Google. Report Abuse - Terms of Service - Additional Terms

Google Forms

Information Gathering for Department or School

Surveys

Social Media Survey

Complete the questions below then click the SUBMIT button.

* Required

Do you have a Facebook, MySpace, Twitter, Pinterest, or Google+ account? *

O Yes

O No

Are your settings private or public? *

O All Private

O Most Settings are Private

O Most Settings are Public

O All Public

O I don't have any accounts

Do you think that having your settings PRIVATE keeps others from seeing your photos? *

O Yes

O No

O I don't have any accounts.

Have you ever tagged other friends in your photos? *

O Yes

O No

O I don't have any accounts.

Student Lesson/Activities

A. C.A.R.P. Website Checklist

Carefully read through and answer each question. Complete the checklist for EACH Website being evaluated. Click SUBMIT when done. - Mrs. Santilio

* Required

Team Names *
First and Last Names

Your answer

1. Title of Web Page or Site *

Your answer

Authority and Accuracy

2. Who is the author of the Website? *
If you find the author or organization name, choose OTHER and type in the name.

○ I couldn't tell.

○ Other:

3. What authorship clues does the URL provide? *

☑ Company (.com)

☐ Academic Institution (.edu)

☐ U.S. Government Agency (.gov)

☑ U.S. Military Site (.mil)

☐ Network of Computers (.net)

☐ Non-Profit Organization (.org)

☐ Country-Specific Site (e.g., .uk)

☐ Personal Web Page (e.g., www.robertsmith.com)

☐ Other:

Classroom Management Forms

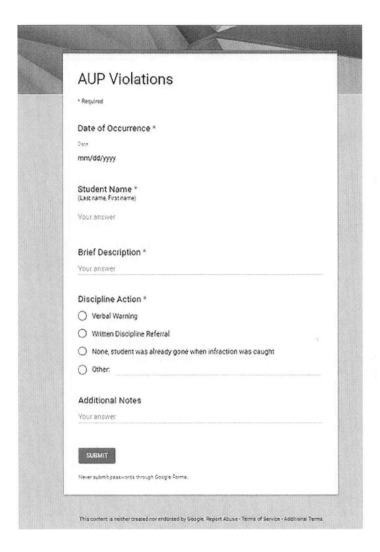

Contests

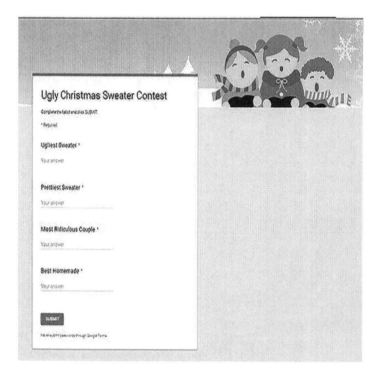

Instructional Mapping

FAQs About Google Classroom

As a teacher, there are a lot of different options that you can use to make the most out of your classroom and you may be curious as to why Google Classroom is the best option to help you out. There are many questions that you may have that pertain to Google Classroom. Some of the questions that you may have about Google Classroom include:

Is it easy to get started with Google Classroom?

Yes, it is really easy to work with Google Classroom, but you do need to remember that it is necessary to have the Google Apps for Education and your domain needs to be verified. We explained how to do this a little bit how to get the Google Apps for Education as well as setting up your domain so make sure that you follow these instructions so that the application can be reviewed right from the beginning.

How are Apps for Education and Classroom connected?

To keep things simple, Google Classroom is not able to work without the help of Google Apps for Education. While you are able to use the Apps for Education all on its own, you will find that using Google Classroom is going to help to make all of it organized and it is much easier to work with. With the help of both the Classroom and Apps working together, both the students and the teachers are able to access the spreadsheets, slideshows, and documents as well as other links without having to worry about attachments and more. Even giving and receiving assignments and grades are easier when these two are combined together.

In addition, there is the option to download the Classroom Mobile app, which will make it easier to access your classes whenever and wherever you would like. This is going to be great for students who are on the go and don't have time to always look through their laptop to see announcements. Even teachers are able to use this mobile app to help them get up assignments and announcements when they are on the go so they can concentrate on other thanks later on.

Does it cost to use Google Classroom?

One of the best things about using Google Classroom is that it is completely free. All you need is a bit of time to help get it all setup, but it will not include any out of pocket costs to make it work. You will have to wait about two weeks in the beginning for your application to be reviewed before you are able to use the class, so consider setting this up early to prevent issues with falling behind.

You will never have to pay for anything when you are using Google Classroom. If you run into a vendor who is asking for you to pay for Google Classroom, you should report them to Google. It is highly likely that this is a fake vendor so do not work with them or provide them with any of your payment information. Google Classroom is, and always will be, free for you to use.

Can I still use Classroom if it is disabled on my domain?

One of the nice things about working with Classroom is that even if it has been disabled on a certain domain, you are still able to use it. With that being said, there are going to be a few restrictions. While you may still be able to get access to a lot of the features, such as Google Drive, Google Docs, and Gmail, you may not be able to see some of the slides, docs, and sheets that were saved in the classroom. It is always best to have your domain turned on when you are working in Google Classroom because this ensures that you are able to use all of the features that are available through the Classroom.

Do I need to have Gmail enabled to use classroom?

It is not necessary to have Gmail enabled in order to use the Google Classroom. You are able to use the Classroom as much as you would like without enabling Gmail, but you would find that you wouldn't be able to receive notifications if the Gmail account isn't turned on. If you would like to have some notifications sent to you, you need to have Gmail enabled.

If you are not that fond of using the Gmail account for this, it is possible to set up your own email server to make it work. This way, you will still be able to receive the notifications that are needed from the Classroom while using the email server that you like the most.

Will I have to work with ads on Google Classroom?

Many people like to work with Google Classroom because they don't have to worry about seeing ads all over the place. Classroom was designed for educational purposes, and

Google recognizes that people don't want to have to fight with ads all of the time when they are learning. You can rest assured that Google and Classroom are not going to take your information and use it for advertising. This is part of the privacy and security that is offered with Google Classroom, which will protect both the student and the teacher from any phishing or spam.

If I have a disability, am I able to use Google Classroom?

Yes, those with disabilities are able to use Google Classroom. Some of the features are not yet complete, but Google is working to make some improvements to classroom so that those who have disabilities can use it too. Aside from using the Screen reader, there are a few other features that you can use with Android including:

BrailleBack: this is a great feature that is going to allow for Braille to be displayed on the Android Device, as long as you have your Bluetooth installed. This is also going to work with the Screen Reader feature that we talked about before. With this feature, you will also be able to input your text while interacting with your Android device.

Switch Access: it is also possible for you to use Switch Access, which is a tool that allows you to control your device with two or more switches. This is great for those who are dealing with limited mobility. It is also a good way to get notifications and alerts.

You are also able to tweak some of the settings that are in Google Classroom in regards to color correction, magnification, captions, touch and hold, using a speaking password, and more.

As you can see, there are a lot of neat things that you are able to do when it comes to using Google Classroom and it is pretty easy for everyone to be able to use. If you ever have some other questions about Google Classroom, you can always contact their support to get the assistance that you need.

Organizing Students Projects

While Google Classroom allows each student to attach multiple artifacts during submission of works, they can now submit all the pieces in one place and have it properly organized for the benefit of the teacher.

- Projects can be set according to assignment options

- For full class projects, send assignments to the entire class

- You can send assignments to multiple classes by selecting the names of the classes you want to see the assignment before you send it

- You can send the assignment to certain individuals to create specific student projects. When creating the assignment, do the following:

  o Deselect all students

  o Select the students that you want to be working on the specific project

  o Send the assignment

- o Only the individual students you selected will receive the assignment

- You can send specific assignments to specific individuals by following the same steps as above

- All the assignments will be organized by students' names, making it easier to keep on top of the assignments and grading.

The Google Classroom allows the teachers to create assignments and assign them to students. When working assignments, the teachers are provided with a number of options. The following steps will help you create an assignment in Google Classroom:

1. Begin by opening the class in which you need to create the assignment.

2. On the class page, click the CLASSWORK tab located at the top.

3. You will see a button written CREATE. Click this button.

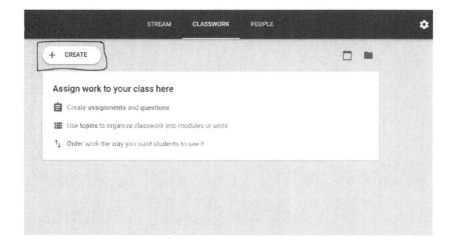

4. After clicking the button, you will see many options showing the items that you can create for the class. Choose "Assignment".

5. A new window will pop up on which you should feed the details for the class. Give a title to the assignment as well as any additional instructions in the next box.

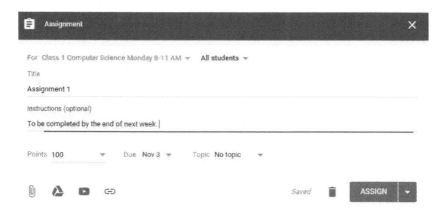

Note that the window also allows you to specify the due date for the assignment as well as the time on the due date by which the assignment should be submitted.

You are also allowed to choose the type of assignment that you need to create. It can be an assignment to all students or to just a selected few of them. You are also allowed to attach files to your assignment. Note that you can get these files from various storages including Google Drive, your computer etc. The file can also be a video file.

4. Once you have filled in all the assignment details, click the "Assign" button to assign the assignment to your students. Once the assignment has been created successfully, you will be notified of the same.

In some cases, you may need to assign the assignment to over 1 class. In such a case, you only have to click on the class name from the top left corner of the window and choose all the classes to which you need to assign the work.

Most teachers who use the Google classroom will prefer to create an assignment from their Drive because this is where most teachers store their resources. However, you will get an advantage when you choose a Drive resource in the Google Classroom, which becomes clear with the options that you get when choosing a file from the drive:

- Students will be able to view the file- you should only choose this option when you need all students to be in a position to view the file, but not to modify it. It is a good option for generic handouts and study guides that the entire class needs access to.

- Students can edit the file- this option should be chosen when you need all students to be able to edit and work on one document. This is good for a collaborative class project in which the students may be working on different slides in a similar Google presentation. It is also well applicable in a situation where the students are all brainstorming on an idea collaboratively to discuss it in the next class.

- Make a copy for each student- when this option is chosen, the Google Classroom will make a copy of the file for each student and give them rights to edit the file. Note that only copies of the original file will be availed to the students but the teacher's master will remain to him and the students will not be granted access to it. This is a good option when you need to distribute a paper with an essay question for students to work on, or where you have a digital worksheet template that you need each student to fill their own answers.

You can also view assignments at any time that you want. This is important as you may need to know the assignment details like the due date. This is possible and it can be done by following the steps given below:

1. Sign into your Google Classroom account.

2. Click the Menu button located at the top. Choose Calendar.

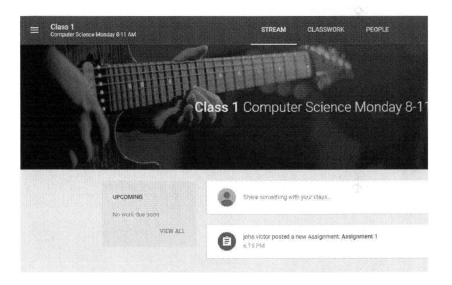

3. You will be taken to a new window with dates. To see either the past or future work, you must use the arrow that is next to date.

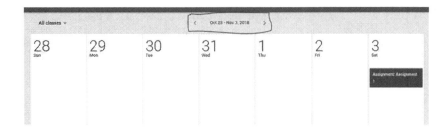

If you need to see all assignments for all your classes, just choose the "All classes" option. If you need to see the assignments for only one class, just click "All classes" then choose the class for which you need to see the assignments.

4. Once you identify an assignment or question that you are looking for, just click to open it.

Organizing Assignments

With Google Classroom, one can now organize the assignments based on their topic. This way, you are able to group the assignments by the unit or classwork from the tab. This is a good way to help students and teachers find the assignment they are looking for more easily.

You can track both your assignments and work using both Google calendar and class calendar. Once a teacher has created an assignment in the classroom, you will be able to see it in both calendars if the account is being used for both calendars.

The following are the steps that will help you create topics in Google Classroom:

1. Navigate to the class.

2. Click the "Classwork" tab to open it.

3. Click the "Create" button.

4. Select "Topic".

5. Give the topic a name and click Add.

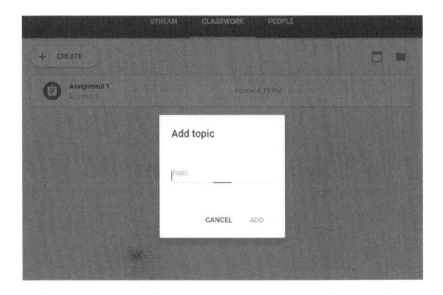

After creating the topic, you will be notified that students are only allowed to see topics with published posts.

You can now add assignments to the topic from the screen for creating assignments. You only have to create the drop-down that is located next to the option for Topic.

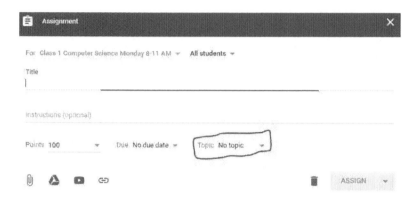

If you have already created the assignment, the following steps will help you assign the assignment to a topic:

1. Click the Classwork tab.

2. Hover over the assignment that you need to move using your mouse.

3. Click on the three dots for More.

4. Select Edit.

5. Identify the drop-down box that is located next to Topic.

6. Click the drop-down then choose the Topic you need to move it to.

7. Once you have assigned the assignment to a topic, click the SAVE button to save the changes you have just made.

How Students Access Assignments

When students log into their accounts, they can see their active assignments by clicking and opening the class that they are part of and viewing all their upcoming assignments. However, there is a quick and easy way to do this. Just click the Menu button located on the top left corner of the screen then choose "To-do" from the menu that pops out.

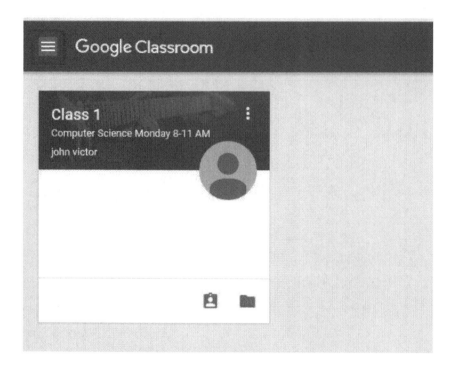

The student will then be able to see all the assignments for his or her classes as well as the ones they have turned in, the outstanding ones and the ones that are overdue. The ones that the teacher has graded will be shown alongside their grades.

Once you click on any of the assignments, the relevant file for the student will be opened. If you dealing with a Google Drive file, an additional button will be added to the toolbar located to the top right corner and close to Share button. The button will be marked "Turn it in". Once you click the button, the assignment will be submitted to the teacher. For the regular assignment, you can submit by clicking the "MARK AS DONE" button.

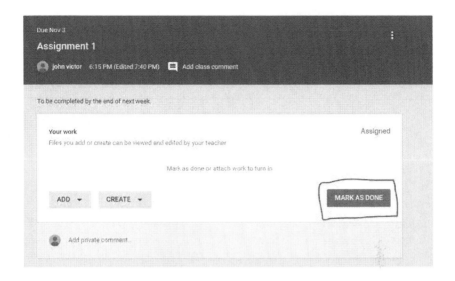

Grading Assignments

There are a different number of ways through which teachers can find submissions from students. The most effective way of doing it is by entering the class that you need to grade then click the name of the assignment from Stream view. If you find that the assignments get lost within the conversations being done by students, look at the sidebar located at the top left of Stream view and you will be able to see the box for "Upcoming Assignments".

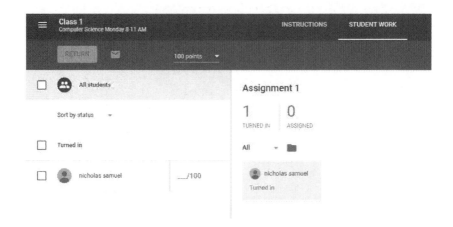

The above figure shows that the student has already turned in the assignment. It is now the work of the teacher to assign the student marks. You can see that the section for marks is assigned __/100.

Identify the assignment that you need to grade then follow the steps given below:

1. Click on the name of the student who submitted the assignment that you need to grade.

2. If the student had attached a document, it will be opened. You can rely on the commenting feature in Drive to give a detailed feedback on the specific parts of the submission made by the student. Once done, close the document. The changes that you have made will be saved automatically.

3. After returning to the classroom, click the box to the right of the student name where it is written __/100. In my case, the total for the assignment is 00 and I want to assign 68 marks to the student. I simply type 68 inside that box. I should now have the following:

4. Ensure that you have checked the box located to the left of the student name then click the "Return" button located at the top of the window. This will save the grade that you have assigned the student. In addition to this, the student will be notified that the assignment they submitted has been graded. After clicking the RETURN button, a new window will pop up asking you to confirm the return to the student. If you have any additional comments to the student regarding the assignment, write them in the provided box. Click RETURN again and the process will continue successfully:

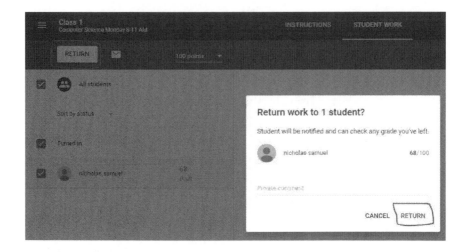

You will also see on the window on the left side the students whom you have graded. In my cases, I have assigned only one student a grade as shown below:

The name of the student as well as the grade assigned is shown in the window.

Grading Tips

Let me answer some of the questions that you may be asking you as far as grading students are concerned:

- Once a teacher has returned an assignment to the student, the teacher no longer has editing rights on the assignment document.

- It is possible for you to return an assignment to a student without grading it by checking the box located to the left of student name and clicking RETURN button. This is important and useful for assignments that have been submitted with an error.

- After returning an assignment, the student gets an email notification about the same.

- You are allowed to change the student's grade anytime you want by clicking the grade then typing in the new grade. Note that this should be done within the same box where we first entered the student grade.

- If you click the folder button, you will be able to open the Google Drive folder in which all the submissions from students have been stored. This can help you when you need to vie all the submitted assignments at once.

- By default, each assignment has a total of 100 points, but this can be changed when click on the drop-down arrow then choose another value or you simply type a value of your own. You can also select the option of not scoring the assignment.

Conclusion

Most of us can recall those moments in our lives when we idly sit in a classroom, but we were not really focused and listening to our teachers. Such scene is still familiar in school settings these days. This traditional method of learning promoted teacher-centered classrooms and give lesser options for students.

We get used by instructors giving us information, students copying what is written on the board, teachers disseminating homework or test papers and the rest of reading and comprehension improvement will be left to the learners.

Although this traditional method could be effective for some students, many of them were forced to be just plain receivers of information instead of motivating them to engage and participate in the learning process.

With the help of technology and assimilation of various applications, a new learning model has developed. The digital era has penetrated our physical classrooms which removes the teacher-centered method of learning.

Learning has now become more collaborative and focuses more on student's progress in the classroom.

Google Classroom indeed, is preparing students for the future. Apparently, we need to know how technology works and by training them young, they will be able to communicate and participate in their careers in the future. The Classroom is helping them to be familiarized and comfortable with the technology.

Google Classroom is also increasing student engagements and keeping them motivated by allowing teachers to motivate them in plenty of ways. Likewise, it gives them the latest information and trend. Web-based contents and materials are also accessible to them. Classrooms all around the world can soon be connected to each other that will broaden information.

For educators, Google Classroom makes it easier for them to deliver instructions while keeping their lesson student-centered. Now they have more time for discussions and answering questions or conducting problem-solving instead of doing and checking homework. Students also have adequate amount of time to understand the subjects.

Immediate assistance from the teacher is a must for students to continually grow and Google Classroom only enhances this aspect. Google Classroom and other learning applications will never replace our teachers, but these tools can help them improve every aspect of learning.

Made in the USA
Middletown, DE
01 July 2020